City Kids &
City Critters!

City Kids & City Critters!

Activities for Urban Explorers

from the Houston Arboretum & Nature Center
by Janet Wier Roberts & Carole Huelbig

Illustrations by Kim Salinas

LEARNING
TRIANGLE
PRESS

An imprint of McGraw-Hill

McGraw-Hill

A Division of The McGraw-Hill Companies

pbk 1 2 3 4 5 6 7 8 9 BBC/BBC 9 0 0 9 8 7 6

Library of Congress Cataloging-in-Publication Data
City kids & city critters! activities for urban explorers /from the
   Houston Arboretum & Nature Center by Janet Wier Roberts & Carole Huelbig;
   illustrated by Kim Salinas
       p.   cm.
   Includes bibliographical references and index.
   ISBN 0-07-053201-X (pbk.)
    1. Urban ecology (Biology)—Study and teaching—Activity programs.
  2. Urban animals—Study and teaching—Activity programs. 3. Natural
history—Study and teaching—Activity programs. I. Roberts, Janet
Wier. II. Huelbig, Carole. III. Houston Arboretum & Nature Center
(Houston, Tex.)
QH541.5.C6C58   1996
574.5'268—dc20   95-52983
                                     CIP

Acquisitions editor: Judith Terrill-Breuer
Editorial team: Robert E. Ostrander, Executive Editor
        Sally Anne Glover, Book Editor
        Jennifer M. Secula, Indexer
Production team: Katherine G. Brown, Director
        Ollie Harmon, Coding
        Janice Ridenour, Computer Artist
        Jan Fisher, Desktop Operator
        Linda L. King, Proofreading
        Linda M. Cramer, Proofreading
Design team: Jaclyn J. Boone, Designer   053201X
        Katherine Lukaszewicz, Associate Designer   LTP1

Acknowledgments

Special thanks to those who contributed their time, advice, and expertise:

❑ The Houston Chapter of the Texas Wildlife Rehabilitation Coalition

❑ The Texas Forest Service—Joe Pase, entomologist

❑ The past and present staff and volunteers of The Houston Arboretum & Nature Center

The Houston Arboretum & Nature Center in Houston, Texas, is an urban wildlife sanctuary for native plants and animals. It educates 10,000 inner-city children annually about the need for protecting wildlife habitats in urban environments.

Contents

Foreword *ix*

Introduction *x*
How to use this book *xii*
Outdoor teaching tips *xiii*

1 Becoming a nature detective 1
Radar ears *3*
Silent stalker *7*
Secret identity *10*
Tell it like it is! *12*
Texture trail *15*
Nosing around *17*
Sensory stroll challenge *20*
Suggested books *23*

2 Observing nature in busy, people places 25
Habitat hunt *26*
Everybody's gotta eat! *29*
Plant power *32*
Plant pursuit game *35*
Food finder survey game *38*
Critter congregations *41*
Wildlife at work *44*
Suggested books *47*

3 Discovering critters in great green spaces 49
Habitat hunt *50*
Great greenery survey *53*
Micro/macro-hike *56*
Insect investigations *60*
Soil sampler *63*
Suggested books *66*

4 Pondering ponds & other wonderful wet places 69
Habitat hunt *70*
Water sampler *73*
Pond zone survey *76*
Amphibians alive! *80*
Creeping crayfish! *84*
Telltale tracks *87*
Suggested books *91*

5 Exploring backyards & schoolyards 93
Habitat hunt *94*
Food factory *97*
Leaf litter critters *100*
Worm world *104*
Caterpillar caper *107*
Bee business *111*
Backyard bird banquet *114*
Suggested books *117*

6 Nurturing nature close to home 119
Habitat helpers *120*
Critter castles *123*
Water ways *126*
Critter cafeteria *129*
Compost casserole *132*
Critter control *135*
Critter care *138*
Suggested books *141*

Resource list 142

Glossary 146

Bibliography 147

Index 149

About the authors 153

Foreword

As we develop areas to better meet the needs of humans, wildlife habitats are often lost in the process. The survival of wildlife habitats depends on the ability of each succeeding generation to appropriately manage environmental change. It is especially crucial that we teach people to identify habitats in urban areas if we expect communities to make responsible decisions that affect wildlife populations. This book serves as an excellent starting point for getting people involved in natural resource conservation.

In an effort to help restore our sense of connection to the environment, many people advocate environmental education. In fact, there seems to be a movement among the educational community toward getting people outdoors, interpreting the environment, and developing outdoor classrooms. In theory, it seems like a step in the right direction. In practice, however, the environmental movement has had limited success in changing the underlying myth that people are separate from the environment—that we are somehow different from all other living things.

This book was written for anyone who has a heart for environmental education but has experienced the frustration of not quite knowing how to do it. Instead of presenting facts and philosophical arguments, the authors present specific methods of engaging young people in observation and understanding. Students learn how to use their senses to develop an awareness of the living things that surround them every day. The reproducible activity guides use common household items and emphasize basic multidisciplinary learning skills. Using these activities, educators can help students develop the capacity to proceed to the more complex environmental issues that face "city kids and city critters" today.

Raymond L. Whitney
Urban Fish and Wildlife Program Leader
Texas Parks and Wildlife Department

Introduction

Ask a child what places she pictures in her mind when she hears people talk about saving "the environment." What places do you picture in your mind? Maybe images of a lush green forest with a flowing stream, a meadow of brightly blooming wildflowers, a deep rock canyon, or a tropical rain forest come to mind. Television, computers, and beautifully illustrated books can transport us to these wild places even if we have never left our hometown. These media color our impressions of what we think is worth saving.

Did an image come to mind of any places in the city where you live or work? The environment we need to save includes our cities, not just beautiful wilderness areas. Have we forgotten that our cities and towns are places where plants and animals seek out space to grow and live—right in the middle of the houses, stores, offices, and other busy places?

As we have built cities, we have taken over wild lands. Wild animals that once lived where cities now grow are challenged to find the food, water, and shelter they need to live and have their young. Some wild animals stay in developed areas and thrive, but others cannot survive there. Animals that are pushed out of their natural habitat must adapt to new food sources and surroundings or die. Migrating animals might only pass through your city. But they must eat, drink, and find a safe place to rest all along their migration route.

Teachers, parents, scout leaders, and outdoor educators using this book will find that the activities show kids the importance of providing habitats for animals in urban areas. Kids will discover that they can help continue the diversity of animal and plant life that is necessary for the balance of life on earth. While wilderness areas do need to be preserved, saving a place for nature near our homes is important, too.

Most children today are growing up in urban areas as "city kids." A connection to the natural world is often lacking. In *The Geography of Childhood—Why Children Need Wild Places*, Gary Paul Nabham and Stephen Trimble write that, "The geography and natural history of childhood begins in family, at home, whether that home is in a remote place or in a city . . . We are concerned about how few children now grow up incorporating plants, animals, and places into their sense of home."

These kid-tested activities from The Houston Arboretum and Nature Center's classes and family programs are designed to guide kids, ages 8 to 12, to discover the natural world near their homes. First the multisensory activities in chapter 1 help children improve their observational skills to become nature detectives. Then they go on "habitat hunts," record city critter observations on reproducible activity sheets, make journals, and do hands-on projects. Locating wildlife in your city can be done during regular daily activities. Watch for animals while working in the yard, riding in the car, taking a walk, picnicking in the park, playing outside at school, or shopping at the mall. Interesting animals are everywhere!

While exploring their urban environment, kids will investigate different types of habitats found in "busy, people places," "great green spaces," "wonderful wet places," and their own backyards or schoolyards. Instead of taking specimens from nature for permanent collections, kids will observe, draw, and photograph animals in their natural setting. Any live specimens collected will be studied and then returned to their habitats. That's a "low-impact" way to study nature. In chapter 6, "Nurturing nature close to home," kids learn to give back to the environment rather than always take.

As children enjoy interacting with the natural world through the activities in this book, they will practice the skills that are important to understanding and applying information and concepts. These skills will enhance their ability to use a scientific process. In each activity, the science process skills that are focused on are noted at the beginning.

This book takes an ecological approach—studying relationships of living things to each other and to their environment. The eco-icons used in the book indicate the ecology concepts explored in each activity. Understanding the interrelationships of all living things teaches respect and wonder for nature, which helps us to make more realistic and responsible decisions concerning use of our natural resources. Once kids find out for themselves about the importance of healthy habitats in their own communities, they will be more likely to make personal choices that will protect the environment for future generations of humans and wildlife.

HOW TO USE THIS BOOK

SHARPEN OBSERVATION
SKILLS
with
CHAPTER ONE
ACTIVITIES
City kids earn
Nature Detective License

↓

EXPLORE, INVESTIGATE, AND
TAKE ACTION

Do activities in
CHAPTERS 2 through 6

↙ ↓ ↘

UNDERSTAND ECOLOGICAL CONCEPTS

An **ecosystem** is the system in which living and nonliving things on earth interact. *Ecology* is the study of these relationships.

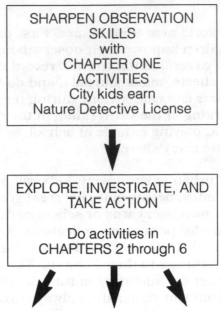

Ecosystem

All living things need a **habitat**—a place to live and find the necessities of life: food, water, shelter, and a place to raise their young.

Habitat

All of the living things in a habitat depend on each other. They live together in an **interdependent community**. Each organism has a job to do. The job and the place where it does it are its *niche*.

Interdependent
community

Biodiversity exists when there are a large number of different kinds of living things in a habitat, making it possible for a community to survive and keep a balance in nature.

Biodiversity

Animals and plants have **adaptations**, which are special features that improve their chances of survival and reproduction.

Adaptations

The energy of the sun gives life to all living things on earth. Energy flows, in the form of food, from one organism to another until it is used up. The path that energy takes from the sun to plant (*producer*), to animal that eats the plant (*herbivore/consumer*), and then to animal that eats the plant eater (*carnivore/consumer*) is called a **food chain**. A *food web* is made up of the complex pattern of different, interconnected paths through which energy travels in a habitat.

Food chain

Nothing in nature is wasted. The **nutrients** (carbon, sulfur, hydrogen, oxygen, nitrogen, and phosphorus), which living things need, move from one organism to another in a never-ending *cycle*. *Decomposers* are the living things that break down dead organisms and make it possible for the nutrients to be reused.

Nutrient cycle

Everything in nature happens in cycles. **Life cycles** are the stages that plants or animals go through during their development.

Life cycles

Outdoor teaching tips

❑ Advise the children about what urban explorers should wear. Long pants and closed-toe shoes keep kids comfortable and safe.

❑ Before going outside, discuss the purpose of the outdoor activity. Focus the group by handing out the activity sheet that will guide their outdoor experience. The time outdoors is a learning time, not recess.

❑ Review specific safety precautions for the area of study.

❑ Remind urban explorers to walk quietly (in a line, with a buddy, etc.) behind the adult leader.

❑ Ask for adult volunteers to accompany the group. An adult at the end of the line will help round up strays! A good ratio is two adults for every 10 kids.

❑ Establish the boundaries. Show the area of study and be clear about what's "off-limits."

❑ Set time limits on the activity, but allow enough time to "smell the roses." Be prepared to abandon your planned activity to take advantage of unexpected discoveries.

❑ Model a sense of wonder and awe at nature. Use the observation skills that you want the kids to learn.

❑ Let the kids make the discoveries.

❑ Let go of the need to name everything in nature.

❑ Model respectful behavior. Leave nature undisturbed.

Becoming a nature detective

An animal relies on its senses to survive. A rabbit has "radar ears" to listen for danger, a mole finds its way underground using its sense of touch, and a snake smells the air with its tongue to sense its prey. Kids would be better equipped to discover the natural world if they could sense things in their environment as well as animals. In this chapter, city kids can become nature detectives and sharpen their own "built-in" observation skills through multisensory games.

Instead of ignoring sights, sounds, smells, and textures of the city, kids will pay more attention to them. Things that went unnoticed before will take on new excitement when their senses are awakened to the surprisingly loud chattering of a tiny chickadee feeding at the top of a tree, the feel of a leaf's velvety underside, or the sight of a brightly colored butterfly refueling on a honeysuckle blossom.

This new sensory awareness will give the nature detectives an advantage when hunting for city critters. Kids will begin to understand that knowing how to describe the living things they find is more important than being able to name them. After practicing the use of sensory skills with these games, kids can earn a nature detective license and checklist, which is at the beginning of this chapter.

NATURE DETECTIVE LICENSE

This license can be earned by doing the activities in chapter 1. To become a nature detective,
kids need to sharpen their senses and improve the observation skills they will use to explore habitats.

---cut and laminate---

OFFICIAL
CITY KIDS AND CITY CRITTERS!
NATURE DETECTIVE LICENSE

_____
Name

is now qualified to observe   school photo
city critters and explore   here
their habitats.

_____
Date

----------------------------- cut here ----------------------------->8---------------------

NATURE DETECTIVE CHECKLIST

Use this **NATURE DETECTIVE CHECKLIST** to record signs of animal life in the different habitats explored in chapters 2 through 5. Use
a new checklist for each place you investigate.

Nature detective's name: _____   Date: _____

Habitat: _____   Weather: _____

EVIDENCE

Check off the evidence you find.
In each box, draw what you see and note where you find it.

_____ insect eggs   _____ holes in the ground   _____ pathways   _____ shed skins

_____ insect egg cases   _____ holes in trees   _____ tracks   _____ sounds

_____ spider eggs   _____ holes in leaves   _____ slime trails   _____ smells

_____ bird eggs   _____ droppings   _____ webs   _____ other . . .

_____ nests   _____ food remains   _____ other . . .   _____ other . . .

Radar ears

Subjects
Science, language arts, art.

Science skills
Observing, comparing and contrasting, recording, predicting results.

Focus
A good sense of hearing and the ability to locate a sound are important adaptations for animal survival. Tuning in to nature's sounds the way animals do can make kids more alert nature detectives. Can you tell what an animal is doing by the sound it is making? Can you tell where the animal is?

Did you know?
A rabbit has "radar ears." Its long ears stand up tall and can swivel to gather sounds from all directions. The rabbit listens for sounds of an approaching predator. By moving its ears backward and forward, it can locate where a sound is coming from without moving its body and drawing attention to itself. Rabbits can listen for danger behind them even while their heads are down nibbling greenery. The rabbit's sensitive ears combined with strong back legs for fast getaways help the rabbit survive.

What you need
❑ Listening Journal
❑ Pencil
❑ Watch or sand timer

What you do

Activity 1

1. Pick a place to go outside and make it your "listening station."

2. Cup your hands behind your ears to make them "radar ears." Push your ears forward with your hands and listen. Now take your hands away from your ears and listen for the difference in volume of the sounds.

3. Now cup your hands in front of your ears to listen to sounds behind you without turning your head. Just like the rabbit, this ear movement helps pinpoint the location of sounds.

4. Experiment with your new "radar ears." Close your eyes for a few minutes to "tune in" to different sounds. Are you able to concentrate better on the sounds when your eyes are closed?

Radar ears

LISTENING JOURNAL

Name _____   Date _____

The best way to sharpen your listening skills is to use them.
Spend 3 minutes listening to your environment and record what you hear.
Listen in the same location at 4 different times of the day.

		ANIMAL SOUNDS	OTHER NATURAL SOUNDS	PEOPLE SOUNDS
MORNING	What did you hear?			
MORNING	What did you see?			
MID-DAY	What did you hear?			
MID-DAY	What did you see?			
EVENING	What did you hear?			
EVENING	What did you see?			
NIGHT	What did you hear?			
NIGHT	What did you see?			

Listening Station location: _____

What did you hear that you didn't expect? _____
_____

What was the loudest sound? _____   What was the quietest? _____

What sounds were the same throughout the day? _____
_____

What sounds did you hear only in the morning? _____

What sounds did you hear only at night? _____

When did you hear the most animal sounds? _____

Activity 2

1. Make a prediction about what you expect to hear at the listening station. Will there be more human-made sounds or animal sounds? What kind of sounds will be heard during the day and at night?

2. Now set your timer for five minutes. Make your "radar ears" and begin listening for sounds.

3. Record the sounds on the listening journal sheet. Make a simple mark for each sound in the journal categories. You might be more specific with notes like "bird," "dog bark," "car horn," "insect buzz," and "wind."

4. If you can see the animal that is making the sound, make notes about its behavior on the back of the sheet.

5. Repeat this activity at four different times of the day, using the same listening station. Make comparisons of your recorded results at that station. Are the sounds the same at each time of day? If not, how were they different? How did the results vary from your predictions?

6. Pick other places for listening stations and repeat the activity. Because of different locations, do you expect different results? Why? What other variables were involved? Did you find that your listening skills improved with practice?

Summary

Listening to nature's sounds can be the first step towards observing and understanding the behavior of animals around you. In everyday life in the city, people usually try to hear less rather than more. They try to ignore sounds like blaring car alarms, whirring weedeaters, whooshing leaf blowers, or roaring airplanes overhead. To be a nature detective, you will need to open your ears again to listen for city critters.

Reading about animal habits will help you locate wildlife in the city. Remember, some animals are active during the day, others at night. Weather is also a factor in the activity of animals. The behavior of animals changes during breeding and nesting as they call for mates, defend their territories, and protect their young. But each animal has a specific way of communicating. Think about how you recognize a friend's voice when she calls on the phone. Even though you can't see the person, you associate the familiar voice with a face in your mind. You have seen her talking before. In the same way, the more you see and hear wildlife in action, the more sounds you will be able to identify in nature.

Following through

Use your listening journal during different seasons and compare the results. Go to your local library or nature center and ask for tapes of wildlife sounds to train your ears for careful listening to sounds in nature. Then try the "radar ears" activity again to see if your listening skills improved. What new animal sounds can you recognize?

Find out more about the way other animals listen. Some grasshoppers have ears on their first pair of legs! Birds have ear holes hidden by feathers. Spiders "hear" with the hair on their legs by picking up vibrations of the web. Some bats make high-pitched squeaks and then use their ears to listen to the echoes that bounce off objects in their path. If it's a building or a power line, the bats avoid it. If it's a flying insect like a moth or mosquito, the bats eat it! What other critters use their listening skills to help them survive in the city?

Silent stalker

Subjects

Science, kinesthetic.

Science skills

Discovering cause-and-effect relationships.

Focus

Listening is a skill that animals need to stay alive. Nature detectives also need to be good listeners and be quiet and patient to get close to critters in the city. Can you walk as silently as a fox? Can you listen like a prey animal?

Did you know?

A red fox often stalks its prey "undercover"—moving secretly in the dark through the undergrowth. Extra fur between the pads of its feet softens the sounds of its footsteps. The fox silently sneaks up and pounces on its prey! With a keen sense of smell, it locates small mammals like rabbits, mice, and squirrels. The fox can even smell a mole burrowing underground near the surface. It creeps up slowly and leaps on the molehill. Hoping the dirt contains the mole, the fox bites and crunches the dirt. Being able to move quietly, combined with its sense of smell and keen hearing, gives the fox an advantage in hunting.

Fox in underbrush

What you need

❑ Small water pistols
❑ Bandannas or cloth for blindfolds
❑ Boundary markers (string)

Before you start

❑ Choose an area for this activity that is away from streets, poles, trees, or other obstacles.

❑ Wear shoes or go barefoot, depending on the safety of the ground surface.

❑ Vary the game by playing at night using narrow-beam flashlights instead of water pistols.

What you do

Activity 1

1. Learn to take "silent stalker steps" like a fox. Start by holding your body upright to keep your balance and look straight ahead instead of down at the ground.

2. Try feeling where you are walking as you take short steps. Lift and place each foot gently, putting one foot almost in front of the other. This narrows your path in the same way that a fox places one paw in front of the other, making an almost straight line of tracks.

3. Instead of heel first, come down on the outside of the foot. Now roll that foot to the inside before putting your weight down. Imagine you have a basketball between your legs if that helps you to walk on the outsides of your feet.

4. Lift the feet with the thighs instead of pushing off with the calves. Crouch down to approach an animal, and keep your arms and hands close to your body.

5. Walk slowly and think like a hunting animal. Listen and move with caution. Blend with the habitat, using the landscape and plants to cover your movements.

Activity 2

1. Play this game with small groups of 2–10 people.

2. Set up the territory boundaries, giving a playing circle of about 20 feet in diameter. If more than one group is playing, be sure the groups are far enough apart so they won't be confused by noise from other groups.

3. Choose a person to be the fox for each group. Remember, everyone will get a turn to be the fox! The fox is the stalking predator looking for its prey.

4. Blindfold the other players and give them a water pistol. Make sure the ears are left uncovered. They are the prey animals and need to be able to hear to "survive!"

5. The predator moves around the territory as quietly as it can, trying to stalk and get close to the prey animals and tag them. The prey move around slowly or position themselves within the territory boundaries.

6. The blindfolded prey listen for the "fox" and squirt water towards any sounds made by the stalking predator. (No fair squirting unless you hear noises! Prey must avoid running out of water because it serves as its defense mechanism.)

7. If the fox gets wet, it has lost its chance to get close enough to catch its prey and goes hungry. A new fox is chosen and the game begins again. The old fox joins the game as a prey animal now.

8. If the fox sneaks up and touches a prey animal, the prey animal is "dead" and must leave the game. The fox then has enough energy from its food that it can continue to hunt until it is heard.

9. For an extra challenge, try stalking on your hands and knees. Can you stalk on your belly?

What if some of the prey animals can't hear as well as others? Try putting cotton in the ears of some of the prey and see which ones survive. Was the outcome predictable?

Summary

Approaching an animal secretly without being heard or seen is hard. When looking for wildlife, this training to be a silent stalker and to pay attention to nature's sounds will make it easier to see more animals. Listening skills are a very important adaptation for animal survival for both predator and prey. Most animals stay alert to guard against being eaten. They often run from noises and hide. The "silent stalker" game demonstrates that to animals, being quiet and listening for sounds can be a matter of life and death! The predator needs to eat to stay alive, and the prey needs to avoid the predator to survive.

Following through

Watch the "foxes" that lived the longest demonstrate their stalking skills to the rest of the group. Practice stalking in different places. Walk through dirt, sand, mud, pine needles, fallen oak leaves, or a puddle. Learn when to stalk. The call of a bird or a sudden movement or noise can put you in stalking mode. Stalk anytime you approach a feeding or watering area. These are often places where an area changes from one type to another—a transition area. Good observation places include edges of forests and fields like golf courses and wooded parks in cities. Shorelines of ponds, lakes, or oceans and banks of rivers and streams where land meets the water are often rich habitats to stalk. Can you think of other good observation places in your city? Practice stalking animals in your own backyard. Another way to observe animals is to move into their area and hide. Remember that animals, especially mammals, might smell you and run away. Experiment with using wind direction to your advantage in watching wildlife. What happens to your scent if you are upwind from the animal you are trying to watch?

Secret identity

Subjects
Science, language arts.

Science skills
Observing, describing, comparing, and contrasting.

Focus
The sense of touch is a valuable skill. To increase the awareness of how things feel, isolate the sense of touch and learn to observe details. Nature has so many different shapes, sizes, and textures. Can you tell what something is just by touching?

Did you know?

A raccoon's forepaws look like a small child's hands. At night, raccoons use their nimble fingers and good sense of touch to find food in places where they cannot see. In muddy water, a raccoon feels around for clams, crayfish, frogs, or fish to eat. Since raccoons are often seen feeling for food on shorelines, people used to think that raccoons always washed their food before they ate it. They are not that picky! Raccoons eat just about anything, including beetles, berries, breakfast cereal, or that uneaten food in your dog's dish. Many city raccoons have found an easy way to make a living. They are able to lift the lid on your garbage can to make a meal of your leftovers. Raccoons can untie string or unlatch a gate. Their sensitive paws give them an advantage, and they have adapted easily to food sources in the city.

What you need
❑ An assortment of different natural and unnatural items
❑ Paper bags (lunch size), 1 per person
❑ Blindfold (optional)
❑ A scorekeeper with paper and pencil

Before you start
❑ Be careful of sharp or pointed edges on the natural items you use.
❑ This is a good indoor activity for rainy days.

Chapter 1

What you do

1. Hide one item in each bag and fold over the top.

2. Each person gets a bag. No peeking! Each person will have a chance to try to identify the secret item in his or her bag by only using the sense of touch like the raccoon.

3. With eyes closed, the first player reaches into the bag to feel the secret item. Don't take the item out of the bag! The player tries to guess what it is and whispers the answer to the game leader. If he is right, he might now peek at the item and begin the next part of the game.

4. Now it's time to see if the rest of the group can guess the secret identity of that player's item. Without naming the item, the player describes the way the item feels to the rest of the group using word clues such as: natural, human-made, rough, smooth, hard, soft, bumpy, ridged, round, straight edges, warm, cool, furry, slick, and so on!

5. Use adjectives to describe the item—not nouns. A scorekeeper will keep track of points for each word clue given. Try to get the group to guess the secret identity of the item with as few clues as possible! At the end of the game, when everyone has had a chance to play, the player with the fewest points is the winner.

Summary

Touching things in nature while exploring helps us connect with the natural world. Some people actually learn best when they can touch what they are studying. Being aware of the variety in nature of sizes, shapes, and textures will help with making scientific observations as nature detectives.

Following through

Learn what not to touch outside, such as poison ivy or oak, stinging caterpillars, and venomous snakes or spiders. Make sure you check for the animals and plants to avoid in your specific area. Enjoy discovering with your hands (and feet), and touch gently as you go exploring with your new skills!

Tell it like it is!

Subjects
Science, language arts.

Science skills
Observing, describing, comparing, and contrasting.

Focus
Being able to make detailed observations is an important skill to develop. Scientists divide animals and plants into groups by observing their differences and similarities. Using close inspection, can you describe and identify what you find in nature?

Did you know?
Most birds are skillful observers with sharp eyesight to help them find food. Some birds eat insects, including flies. But the syrphid fly has black and yellow stripes and looks like a bee. A bird is not as likely to eat a fly that looks like a bee, so the fly's chances of survival are improved. At first glance you might mistake the fly for a bee, too. But if you look closely, the flies have only one pair of wings while the bees have two pairs.

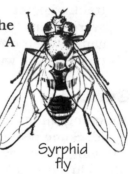

Syrphid fly

What you need
(1 per person):
- ❑ Nature items that are alike, such as pine cones, oranges, nuts
- ❑ Many natural objects that are different, such as shells, various kinds of pine cones, various flowers, leaves, feathers, fur, snake skin, bones, rocks, crystals, etc.
- ❑ A scorekeeper with pencil and paper (for Activity 2)

Before you start
- ❑ Be careful about prickly or sharp edges on the natural items.

What you do

Activity 1

1. Start with the nature items that are alike. Put them on a table for everyone to observe.

2. Each person picks one of the objects. If oranges are being used, each person will have one orange.

3. Each person takes 1 minute to inspect his or her object and then places it back in the center of the table.

4. Everyone closes their eyes while the objects are rearranged.

5. Take turns sorting through the objects. Can each person find his or her specimen?

For an extra challenge, kids can try to find their object with their eyes closed!

Activity 2

1. Now use the natural objects that are different. Each person is given one object to hold.

2. Form a circle with each person in the group seated and facing the inside of the circle.

3. Choose a person to begin the game. That person says one word to describe his or her object, then hands it to the next person in the circle. In turn, each person in the circle must say a new word to describe that same item.

4. With the paper and pencil, a scorekeeper keeps track of the descriptive words as they are used so there are no repeats for that item. Each person gets a point for the word he or she uses. If someone repeats a word choice, the person loses a point, but he or she can try again on the next "go-'round." After going around the circle once, if players want to continue that item in play, they can earn a point for each additional word they give to describe the item.

5. Now the next person in the circle describes his or her object with one word. The game continues around the circle until each object has been "in play."

6. Which object was the most difficult to describe? Who had the most word points?

Summary

To appreciate and connect with nature, take the time to look closely. This game encourages practice in observing and describing details. The ability to see small differences or note changes helps with nature study.

Think about how wild animals see our shared world. Most mammals cannot see bright colors. They see pale shades of gray. Their eyes are designed to spot movement. Predatory animals like the coyote or house cat have eyes facing forward, which helps them focus and judge the distance and location of their prey. Prey animals usually have eyes on the sides of their heads. While standing still, prey animals can see in front, to the side, and behind—without giving away their location. Have you ever noticed how a fly's eyes bulge out from its head? Like most adult insects, the big compound eyes are made of many tiny lenses that let the fly see above, behind, and below at the same time. How do you think that helps the insects? Snails have eyes on long stalks. Their eyes can recognize light and dark. This ability helps them find

Tell it like it is!

cover and know whether it is day or night. As you explore and discover animals around you, find out more about the way they view their habitat.

Following through

Learn more about how animals are alike and different. Pick an animal and find out its scientific classification. Read about animal mimicry. Some animals survive by looking like something else. The harmless milk snake has similar coloration to the venomous coral snake. The caterpillar of the giant swallowtail butterfly looks like a bird dropping! Who wants to eat that?

The leaf hopper's body shape and color mimic the thorns of a plant, making it hard for a predator to see. Even as a nature detective, it's easy to be fooled. With careful observation, describe and record what you see. Then compare and contrast it to other living things to identify the animal or plant you are studying.

Texture trail

Subjects
Science, language arts, art.

Science skills
Observing, comparing and contrasting, recording, sequencing.

Focus
Experiencing nature through the sense of touch allows us to gather useful information about the world around us. Search outside to discover textures and patterns in nature. Can you navigate by using your sense of touch?

Did you know?
A mole's eyes are buried in the soft fur of its face and are not much bigger than the head of a pin. The mole can see little more than the difference between bright sunlight and darkness. Its eyes are of no use in hunting insects and earthworms underground. This little furry critter navigates and finds food underground by using its excellent sense of touch. With a sensitive snout and specialized sensory hairs on its front feet and tail, it feels its way along the soil tunnels it digs. A mole can feel vibrations through the ground as a predator or human approaches. The mole's sense of touch warns it when to dig down deeper to safety.

Mole

What you need
❑ Sheets of typing paper or unprinted newspaper
❑ Crayons (with paper wrapping removed)
❑ Hole punch
❑ Thin ribbon or yarn
❑ Cloth or bandannas for blindfolds (optional)

Before you start
❑ Remove any hazards from the area where you plan to make your trail.
❑ Check out the area for poison ivy or poison oak.
❑ Watch out for thorns in bushes (ouch!).

What you do
(This activity works well individually or in pairs.)

Activity 1

1. Punch three holes in the sheets of paper to make your own notebook for your texture journal. Use ribbon or yarn threaded through the holes to tie it together.

2. Go outside with your texture journal and crayon. Search all around for interesting textures you can see and feel.

3. Record the textures in your texture journal by making rubbings. Put your paper over the things you find and rub over each one with the side of the crayon. Try it with things like the underside of a leaf, tree bark, rocks, wood, or the sole of your shoes!

4. Make notes about each item. What is it? Living or nonliving? Where was it? What shapes and patterns do you notice in nature?

Activity 2

1. Now working with a partner, each of you will make a texture trail map. (Make sure your partner isn't watching you make your map!)

2. Choose a pathway. Walk along and find textures to record on separate sheets of paper.

3. Number the texture trail map pages in sequence.

4. Give the texture trail map to your partner. See if your partner can follow your texture trail after studying the map.

Summary

Touching natural things—living and nonliving—helps us connect to the natural world. What new things did you notice? Which things surprised you? We can become more aware of our surroundings by reawakening the sense of touch. Children might need permission and encouragement to touch things because they have become conditioned by warnings of "Don't touch!" or "Be careful!"

Following through

Try touching some of the natural things with your feet instead of your hands. Make a texture journal of what you find when you are crawling on your hands and knees.

How is the experience different this time? Plan a "messy day" outdoors and celebrate the joy of sand, water, and mud. Wear old clothes and experience how these natural elements feel with your whole body!

Nosing around

Subjects

Science, language arts.

Science skills

Observing, comparing, and contrasting.

Focus

The sense of smell plays various important roles in the survival of animals. Some animals depend on their sense of smell to find food, mates, or territory boundaries and identify their young. Nature detectives, could you isolate and identify specific smells in your "habitat" if your survival depends on it?

Did you know?

Moths have the best sense of smell in the animal world. Like many other types of animals, moths use scents to attract a mate. In insects, these scents are called *pheromones*. When a female moth is ready to breed, she smells different than before. With its big, feathery antennae, a male moth can smell a female's scent from several miles away. He follows the scent in the air and flies to the female to mate. This strong dependence on its sense of smell can be the key to the moth's survival or its downfall. Some moths (as caterpillars) are considered crop pests. Scientists have been able to develop a nontoxic pest control method by understanding the moth's use of chemical scents as attractants. By confusing male moths with fake pheromones, the males are attracted to the wrong place. If they can't find a female, they cannot breed and their life cycle is broken. Farmers will then have less crop damage from new moth caterpillars.

Moth

What you need

- ❑ 35 opaque containers with 3 holes poked in each lid (paper cups with aluminum foil tops or empty 35-mm film canisters)
- ❑ Cotton balls
- ❑ 5 different scents, such as food flavoring extracts, potpourri oils, or food products like a glob of peanut butter, slice of an orange, an onion, a banana, or herbs
- ❑ 5 shoe boxes
- ❑ Tape
- ❑ 30 3-×-5 note cards

Before you start

Activity setup

❑ Hide the scents in the containers ahead of time so the players cannot watch. Soak cotton balls in the extracts or oils unless you are using food products.

❑ Make 7 containers of each of the 5 scents. Keep each scent set in a separate shoe box. (All onion containers in one shoe box, all banana containers in another, and so on.)

❑ Use one sentence (see the following list) for each scent set. Divide each sentence into 6 parts. Write the sentence parts on a 3-×-5 card. Tape a card on each container in a scent set. Do this for only 6 sets; one will be left over. Survival strategy sentences:
  • Coyotes say "Do not enter" by marking territories with their scent.
  • Salmon follow smells up rivers to their birthplace to lay eggs.
  • Seals find their babies in a crowd by sniffing their scent.
  • Turkey vultures use their sense of smell to find the dead animals they eat.
  • Snakes smell the air with their tongue to sense their prey or find a mate.

❑ Set up 6 "smelling stations" on a path or trail at intervals of about 50 feet. At each station there will be 1 container of each of the 5 scents. You will now have 1 container of each scent left over to use for the players as a reference guide.

What you do

(This works best with 5 players or more.) Play this game and find out how some animals survive using their sense of smell. At the end of the game, if players have identified the smells correctly, they will have collected all the word cards and will be able to make a complete "survival strategy" sentence.

1. Divide the group into 5 "smell squads." Assign each smell squad one of the scents to follow. Each squad can carry its reference scent container when it goes nosing around.

2. The smell squads follow the path, stopping at each smell station to sniff the containers.

3. When the squad finds its own scent, the squad collects the card attached to that container.

4. After visiting all 6 smell stations, the squads will have collected cards from all their scent containers.

5. To make sure they followed their noses to the correct scents, the smell squad then tries to unscramble the cards to make a complete sentence.

6. If they identified their scent containers correctly, their sentence will reveal an animal survival strategy that uses smell. Each smell squad shares its sentence with the whole group.

Summary

Animals can't talk, but some have an increased sense of smell and use it as a way of communicating. Most mammals have a much more developed sense of smell than humans. Your dog's sense of smell is about five times stronger than yours. Scents can be thought of as signals. Nature detectives can put their noses to work sniffing out valuable clues to find city critters. The smell of blooming flowers is a signal that insects will be nearby. The smell of a dead animal can be a clue that leads a nature detective to beetles, flies, and crows.

Following through

Find out about how other animals use their sense of smell. Is it the size of an animal's nose that gives it a good sense of smell? Do critters sense smells in other ways besides through their nose? Observe some busy sidewalk ants. They touch and smell things with their two long antennae. Ants can sense sounds, flavors, and odors through these "feelers."

Sensory stroll challenge

Science skills

Observing, recording, comparing, and contrasting.

Focus

Scientists must first learn to make observations before they can make new discoveries. As a nature detective, you'll put all of your sensory skills to work. How many of these sensory experiences can you have in your neighborhood or schoolyard?

Did you know?

Many animals have keener senses than people. Their sense organs have developed to suit how and where they live. Hawks are keen-eyed, daytime hunters that can see eight times better than humans! Owls hunt at night but have big eyes that can see in dim light. Their ears can hear faint sounds like a mouse rustling through the leaves on the ground. Another night hunter, the little brown bat, depends on its ears instead of its eyes. Bats find their way in the dark by making high-pitched sounds and listening to the echoes that bounce off objects. By using this specialized listening ability called *echo-location*, bats can find flying insects to eat. One brown bat can eat 600 mosquitoes in one hour!

What you need

❑ A penny
❑ Sensory Stroll Challenge Activity Sheet
❑ A pencil

Before you start

❑ Have towels ready; this might get messy!

What you do

(This activity can be done individually or in pairs.)

1. Go outside and find a starting point for your sensory stroll. Walk to the intersection of a street or nature trail.

2. Flip your penny once. If the penny lands on "heads," go right. If it lands on "tails," go left.

SENSORY STROLL CHALLENGE ACTIVITY SHEET

Name _____   Date _____

Check off each sensory activity you are able to complete.

Hug a tree.

Sift dirt through your fingers.

Listen for an animal's warning sound.

Let a worm wiggle in your hand.

Lct a slug slide over your hand.

Listen to a bird's song

Feel a breeze.

Chase a butterfly.

Squish mud through your toes.

Crush a leaf and smell it.

Jump in a puddle.

Listen to the rain.

Smell a flower.

Feel the warmth of the sun.

Listen to the wind.

Hear the hum of insects.

3. As you go, check off the Sensory Stroll challenges you are able to complete. Continue to use the penny to decide which way you will go next.

4. How many challenges did you do? Compare your sheet with others. Whose path lead to the most experiences? Did certain areas offer more variety of experience? If so, why?

Following through

What's different about your results when you do the sensory stroll in the evening or at night?

Suggested books

Brown, Jr., Tom. 1983. *Field Guide to Nature Observation and Tracking*. New York: Berkley Books.

> This is an in-depth description of ways to read animal signs and tracks. Brown gives advice on how to sharpen one's senses to observe all kinds of wildlife.

Brown, Jr., Tom. 1983. *The Tracker*. New York: Berkley Books.

> Tom Brown tells an interesting story about an elderly Native American who taught him how to observe and track all kinds of animals.

George, Jean Craighead. *All Upon A Sidewalk*.

> A story about an ant's adventures as it follows chemical signals to find a reward.

Kohl, Judith and Herbert. 1977. *The View From the Oak*. San Francisco: Sierra Books.

> This book explores the many different ways animal species sense their world.

Nabhan, Gary Paul and Stephen Trimble. 1994. *The Geography of Childhood, Why Children Need Wild Places*. Boston: Beacon Press.

> An exploration of how children relate to and observe their natural environment.

Robertson, Kayo. 1986. *Signs Along a River*. New York: Roberts Rinehart Inc.

> Read this book to children as a way to inspire them to use their senses to read nature like a book in which the words are animal tracks and signs left behind.

Suzuki, David. 1986. *Looking at Senses*. New York: John Wiley & Sons.

> Suzuki's book is a thorough explanation of our five senses and how they compare to other animal species, with many good suggestions for experiments.

Van der Meer, Ron. 1990. *Amazing Animal Senses*. Boston: Little, Brown and Co.

> An interesting comparison of many different animal senses.

Wright, Rachel. 1989. *Look at Eyes, Ears and Noses*. New York: Franklin Watts.

> Learning about the excellent senses of many animals will inspire your young naturalists to sharpen their own senses.

Observing nature in busy, people places

2

People began building cities only about 5,000 years ago. As people built structures and took over more wild land, most of the wildlife had to move over! Some animals moved into the surrounding countryside if that habitat suited their needs. When kids observe nature in the city, they will see that some animals originally adapted to live in wild places have gotten used to the activity in busy, people places and can thrive in the city.

Some living things take advantage of what cities have to offer. Cities have food sources, open spaces, and nooks and crannies to live in, buildings to roost on, and underground storm sewers to breed and travel in. Trees planted by people for shade and beauty also provide shelter and food for many city critters like bats, blue jays, and beetles. Some plant species grow better in sidewalk cracks because the soil is made more alkaline by the lime that dissolves out of the concrete. Purple martins actually prefer to be near people places when they nest.

What unnatural nooks do animals use when their natural shelters are not available? What food and water sources do cities provide? What jobs do urban plants and animals do? How can we help wildlife in the city? Remember to use your nature detective checklist to search for evidence of city critters in places all around town.

Habitat hunt

Subjects
Science, math.

Science skills
Observing, comparing and contrasting, recording.

Focus
Animals need certain habitats to survive. That's the place they are best suited to find food, water, shelter, and space to raise their young. What critters have adapted to live in the center of your city?

Did you know?

Peregrine on ledge

The peregrine falcon is a bird that was threatened with extinction by the 1970s. The pesticide DDT caused the falcon's eggs to weaken, and baby birds never hatched. Now DDT use has been banned and people are working to help falcons through breeding and release programs. After falcon chicks are hatched in captivity, they are released into the wild. Some are put on skyscraper ledges in the middle of busy downtowns in the United States and Canada! Why? Skyscraper ledges make as good a site for their nests and lookouts as cliffs do in the wild. From there, they can swoop down at almost 200 mph to prey on pigeons and other city birds. Because of these advantages, some adult peregrine falcons have chosen building ledges for nest sites by following their instincts and adapting to what the city can provide.

What you need
❑ Habitat Hunt Checklist
❑ Pencil
❑ Binoculars (optional)

What you do
1. Urban explorers take the Habitat Hunt Checklist on a downtown outing or a trip to busy, people places. Close adult supervision—one adult for every two or three children—is advised.
2. Look for city spaces used by animals as nest sites, lookouts, or hunting and feeding or sleeping spots.
3. Compare the spaces made by people to natural places in the wild. How do they match? For instance, how is a traffic light pole like a hollow branch of a tree? How is an overpass like the rocky ledge of a cliff?
4. Are there any advantages for the animals that live in the city? Where are most of the animals found? What food and water is nearby? What time of day was best for observations? What threats and dangers do animals face in busy, people places?

HABITAT HUNT CHECKLIST

Urban explorer's name _____   Date _____

Explore downtown or take a trip through the city.
How many of these "unnatural nooks" can you find? What city critters use them?
Compare these places made by people to natural places. How do they match?
What food and water is nearby?

BUSY, PEOPLE PLACES	CITY CRITTERS	-NATURAL PLACES -FOOD -WHEN ACTIVE
In storm drains	rat	-Underground burrow -eats grain, people's leftovers -nighttime
in traffic lights	starling	-treeholes, other cavities -eats bugs, worms, seeds, leftovers -daytime
on flat roofs	nighthawk	-gravel beaches, barren fields -eats flying insects -dusk, nighttime
on building ledges	peregrine falcon	-cliffs, rock outcrops -eats pigeons, sparrows, blackbirds -daytime
under bridges	bat	-caves, natural overhangs -eats flying insects -nighttime
under bridges	barn swallow	-natural overhangs, rock cliffs -eats flying insects -daytime
under freeway overpasses	pigeon	-rock cliffs and ledges -eats seeds, bugs, people's leftovers -daytime
in sidewalk cracks	ant	-underground burrows -dead animals -daytime
around street lamps	bat and insect	-trees, caves -bat eats insects; moth eats nectar -nighttime
utility poles	American kestral	-treetops -eats snakes, birds, grasshoppers -daytime

Summary

Animals follow their instincts in choosing a place for shelter or a place to nest. Cities offer a variety of spaces to substitute for the "real thing." Seasonal changes, the time of day that observations are made, and food supply will make a difference in the critters seen. People's lifestyles have an effect on animal habitats. Some habitats are created while others are destroyed. For many animals, the city is a safer place to live than in the wild because there are fewer large predators.

Taking advantage of city spaces and food supplies, some southern birds and mammals such as armadillos, opossums, cardinals, and mockingbirds have been extending their ranges northward and becoming residents in cities and towns.

Following through

Write to the Peregrine Fund, Inc., 5666 West Flying Hawk Lane, Boise, ID 83709, to find out if peregrine falcons are being helped in or near your city. Contact some of the conservation organizations in the resource list at the back of this book to find out if there are any endangered animals in your area. If they aren't residents, do they migrate through the area? Animals instinctively take migration routes that were determined by their ancestors. But many urban areas now exist where there used to be wild land. Does your city do a good job yielding to habitats for migrating animals like songbirds, hummingbirds, or butterflies?

Everybody's gotta eat!

Subjects
Science, math.

Science skills
Predicting, discovering cause and effect.

Focus
In the city, where people have changed the natural surroundings, finding enough food can be hard for wildlife. If you were a bird, could you find the type of food you need and get enough of it to survive?

Did you know?
Each fall at least two-thirds of the birds in North America migrate several hundred miles to find food. When days grow shorter, over 100 species of birds, including insect-eating warblers and seed-eating finches, fly south to tropical habitats where food is more plentiful. Some travel as far as 2000 miles! Even tiny hummingbirds go as far as Mexico or South America to sip nectar from flowering plants. Many of these birds fly 550 miles across the Gulf of Mexico without stopping to get to their winter habitat. Then they fly back to North America in the spring to nest and raise their young. Habitat protection in North, Central, and South America is a must for the survival of migratory birds.

Ruby-thoated hummingbird

What you need
❑ Colored popcorn or cereal as "bird food"
❑ A watch or minute timer
❑ Clipboard with paper
❑ Pencil

Before you start
❑ Set game area boundaries (about 40 ft. × 40 ft.).
❑ Avoid areas with long grass where popcorn or cereal can hide!
❑ Count 100 of each color: orange, yellow, red, blue, and green "bird food" pieces.

What you do
Round 1
1. For this game, each child pretends to be a migrating bird passing through town in a flock.

Everybody's gotta eat!

2. Each bird's job is to find 20 pieces of food within the game area, which is its "habitat."

3. Scatter all the pieces of colored "food" randomly around the birds' "habitat."

4. The hungry birds begin "feeding" in the "habitat" for two to three minutes. Just as real birds have different ways of getting and carrying their food, the players might carry the colored food any way they can except in their mouths (for safety reasons). Using a pocket or stuffing it in their shoes could be a feeding advantage!

5. After two to three minutes, the birds stop "feeding." Did each bird get enough to survive? Each bird counts the numbers of each color that it collected. The flock then totals the numbers of each color and plots the results as a bar graph using the paper, pencil, and clipboard.

6. Based on the color count, what color berries or seeds would be an advantage to plants that depend on animals to scatter their seeds? (Hint: Birds have color vision.)

Round 2

1. Children return to the habitat pretending to be a second flock of hungry migratory birds.

2. Repeat the game again to see who survives. Graph the collected colors again.

3. Did it take longer for the later flocks to find food? Did fewer survive? Depending on the size of the flocks, the game might need to be played several times to illustrate that resources in a habitat can be depleted, which leaves latecomers with little choice.

4. How does nature select for the healthiest individuals to survive and reproduce? With migratory birds, usually the stronger fliers get first choice of available food that is easier to find so they have enough energy to travel to nesting sites.

Summary

Ancient migratory pathways are still followed by animals, even though cities might stand where wild places once offered plentiful feeding grounds. Nature's changing conditions alone can challenge an animal's ability to find foods. While life near humans might provide some unique food sources, many natural foods become harder to find. Habitat loss is a major reason that animals become endangered or extinct.

Following through

Animals with specialized beaks or mouth parts and strict feeding habits are more limited in food choices, making it more difficult to survive. Play the "Bird Beak Adaptation" game available from the National Wildlife Federation's "NatureScope—Birds." Using range maps in a field guide to birds, find out what birds migrate through your city. To find out more about saving habitats for migratory birds in your area, contact:

Partners in Flight
Peter Stangel
National Fish and Wildlife Foundation
1120 Connecticut Ave. N.W., Suite 900
Washington, DC 20036

Plant power

Subjects
Science, math.

Science skills
Predicting, recording.

Focus
Plants are part of every habitat. Some city plants have adapted to grow in the most unusual places—such as the crevice in a building wall or in a tiny crack in the sidewalk. How do plants do that?

Did you know?
Some plants grow right up through hard clumps of soil or rocks as they reach for the sun. Sometimes the rocks and clumps break into smaller pieces as the plant grows larger. Then water, wind, and ice wear down the clumps and rocks into even smaller bits, which eventually become new soil. The growth power of plants plays a part in making soil.

What you need
For each person:
- ❏ 2 rocks
- ❏ 3 clear plastic cups (16 oz.)
- ❏ Potting soil and water
- ❏ 8 sunflower seeds
- ❏ A permanent marker, pencil, paper, and ruler
- ❏ Plant Power Activity Sheet

Before you start
❏ A botanist is a scientist who studies plant life.

What you do
1. Each botanist marks 3 cups with his or her name and numbers them 1, 2, and 3.

2. Fill the cups with potting soil.

3. Plant one seed about ½ inch "underground" in cups #1 and #2.
   In cup #3, plant 6 seeds close together in the center of cup at ½-inch depth.

4. Now place a rock on top of the soil in cup #1 and cup #3.
   Cup #2 has no weight placed over the seed.

5. Water the seeds daily, but don't drown them!

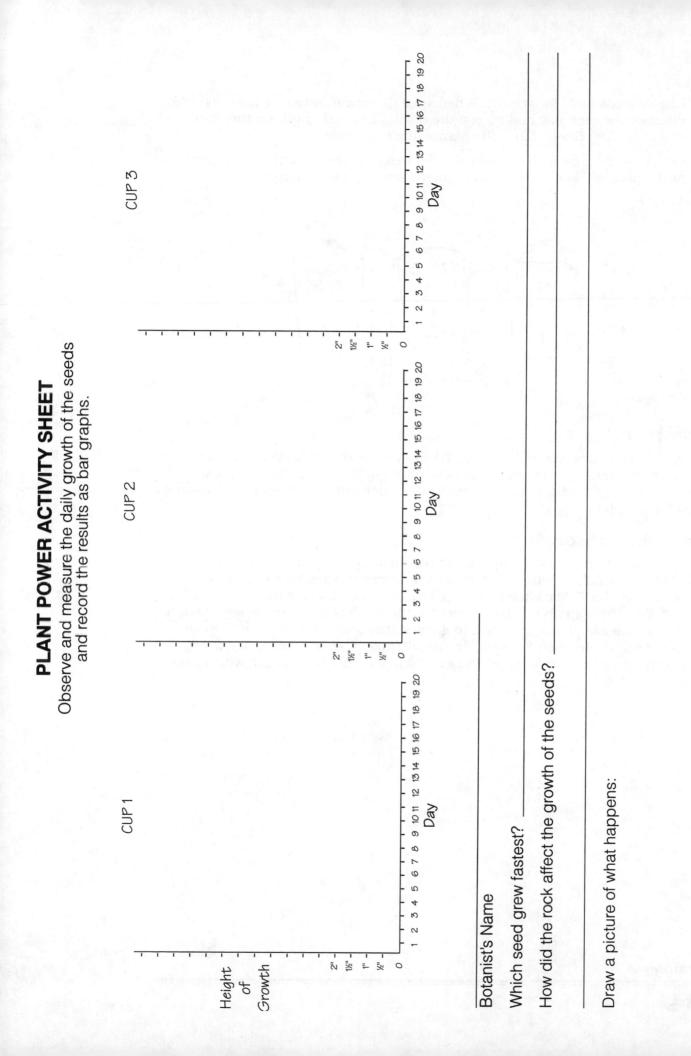

PLANT POWER ACTIVITY SHEET

Observe and measure the daily growth of the seeds and record the results as bar graphs.

CUP 1

Height
of
Growth

2"
1½"
1"
½"
0

1 2 3 4 5 6 7 8 9 10 11 12 13 14 15 16 17 18 19 20
Day

CUP 2

2"
1½"
1"
½"
0

1 2 3 4 5 6 7 8 9 10 11 12 13 14 15 16 17 18 19 20
Day

CUP 3

2"
1½"
1"
½"
0

1 2 3 4 5 6 7 8 9 10 11 12 13 14 15 16 17 18 19 20
Day

Botanist's Name _____

Which seed grew fastest? _____

How did the rock affect the growth of the seeds? _____
_____

Draw a picture of what happens:

6. Check seeds daily for growth. When sprouts appear, measure how high the plants grow each day and record the results as a bar graph on the Plant Power Activity Sheet. Move the plants to a sunny area.

7. Which seeds grew fastest? How did the weight of the rock affect the growth of the plants? How does this growing power help plants survive?

Seed cup setup

Summary

Even though young plants look delicate, they have strength. Water rising up through the roots spreads to the growing parts of the plant. The plant can push up through the soil and as new leaves reach sunlight, they begin making food for the plant.

Following through

Do the "Plant Pursuit Game" in this chapter to see plant power in action outside. In the fall, look for different seed travelers outside. How did the seeds get where they are? Mark the seed's spot in the fall and revisit the site in the spring. Was the seed able to grow there? If not, think of the reasons why. Did the seed have everything it needed to grow in that spot? Did an animal eat the seed—or carry it to another place? In the fall, take a "sock walk" to see which seed travelers hitch a ride. Plant the sock in a pot, water it, and see what grows!

Plant pursuit game

Subject

Science.

Science skills

Observing, recording.

Focus

Plants are the only living things that can make food from the energy of the sun. Many animals get their energy from eating plants, so to attract wildlife, cities need a variety of plants. Plants also provide shelter and give off oxygen that wildlife and people need. How many different plants can you find in busy, people places?

Did you know?

Plants have evolved in surprising ways to spread their seeds. The seeds travel to places away from the parent plant where they have room to grow. Maple and pine tree seeds have wings, lotus seed pods float like boats, dandelion seeds have parachutes, and some seeds travel with animals—on their fur or inside their bodies. Seeds that have been eaten might pass through an animal's stomach undigested and are then deposited with their droppings— often far away from the parent plant.

Concepts

What you need

❑ Pencil
❑ Plant Pursuit Game sheet

Before you start

❑ Avoid poison ivy and poison oak.
❑ Instead of collecting plant specimens, draw pictures, take photographs, or make notes.

What you do

1. With the Plant Pursuit Game Sheet and pencil, go on a prowl for plants.

2. Search in downtown business areas, a shopping center, or other busy places to discover different kinds of plants surviving in unlikely places.

3. Record the type of plants that are found and earn extra points for the diversity that is discovered.

Summary

With "plant power" working to push stems up through cracks or roots down into hard soil, some plants seem able to grow wherever their seeds have

PLANT PURSUIT GAME SHEET

_____   _____
Botanist's name   Habitat location

★ Earn 1 point for each type of plant or plant product found.
★ Get double points for plants in unusual places.

 check off when seen   ★ Get triple points for plant to plant interactions.

grasses 1	nuts 1	lichen 1	pine cone 1
vine growing on tree 3	roots pushing up sidewalk 2	flower nectar 1	evergreen tree 1
dandelion 1	tubular flower 1	tree shading other plants 3	plant on side of building 2
plant pollen 1	seed with parachute 1	seed with 2 wings 1	plant in freeway cracks 2
moss 1	oak tree 1	plant in cracks/crevices 2	crab grass 1
plants in parking lots 2	seed with one wing 1	leaves from deciduous tree 1	other 1
flowering tree 1	cone-bearing tree 1	other 1	other 1

Tally your score: _____   Try this in other places and compare your scores.

Scoring example: If moss is in a crack, double the points. If it is found on a tree, triple your points.
If vine is not found growing on a tree, you get only 1 point.

landed. Plants in unlikely places don't need rich soil or much space to live. Whatever rain falls is enough water for them. They are urban survivors.

Because living things depend on each other, they interact with each other. Did you see plant-to-plant interactions like a large plant shading a small plant or a vine or lichen growing on a tree? Animal-to-plant interactions might be easier to notice. Squirrels depend on trees for food, shelter, and protection. A forgotten acorn buried by a squirrel might grow into another oak tree. That one oak tree might provide hundreds of critters with food and shelter. At least 96 species of birds and mammals are known to use acorns as an important food source. Butterflies, bees, and hummingbirds pollinate flowers, which help the plant to make seeds. Other animals spread the seeds of plants when they eat berries or fruits. Violets depend on earthworms to keep the soil loose and fertile and rely on trees for shade. A rabbit might nibble those violets for dinner. Interactions are everywhere!

Following through

Learn how to recognize poison ivy and poison oak plants. The oils contained in the roots, stems, leaves, and berries can cause an itchy skin rash on humans, and yet the plants provide wildlife with food and shelter. About 75 species of animals use the poison ivy plant as a food source. When birds eat the berries, they scatter the poison ivy seeds in their droppings. Even though some plants are unpopular with people, they are important in the balance of nature.

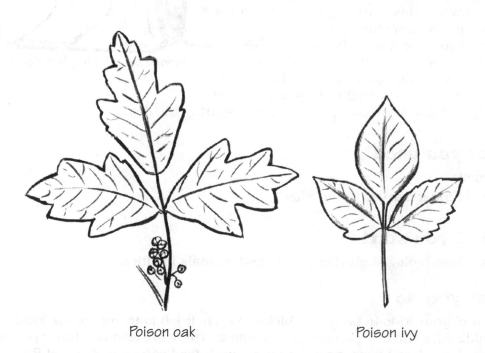

Poison oak   Poison ivy

Food finder survey game

Subjects
Science, social studies.

Concepts

Science skills
Observing, predicting, recording.

Focus
To live, animals must find food in their habitat. Where you find food, you're more likely to be able to observe animals. What kind of food do critters find in your city?

Did you know?
Some city critters have adapted to substitutes for their natural food. When honeybees sip sugary drips in soda cans, they can do with fewer flowers. Has your dog ever seemed really hungry in the morning even though you gave it food the night before? Opossums and raccoons might have feasted on your dog's food in the backyard during the night. Jays and sparrows might steal dry dog food—piece by piece—during the day!

Honey bee sipping from soda

What you need
❑ Pencil
❑ Food Finder Survey Game Sheet

Before you start
❑ An urban biologist studies plants and animals in cities.

What you do
1. "Hire" your kids to be urban biologists. Their job is to survey the local wildlife for the city planning department. There are animals that are seed snackers, bug biters, nectar sippers, junk-food eaters, and more! By looking for available food sources, urban biologists can predict which animals could survive in their city.

2. The urban biologists take the food finder survey sheet on any city outing. Some observations can be made from a bus or car.

FOOD FINDER SURVEY GAME SHEET

_____   _____
Urban biologist's name   Habitat location

Take a look in busy, city places to find food sources for city critters.
Which animals would be able to survive in your city?
As you do the survey, check each box when you find that food.
How did your city do? 1-7 _____ poor   8-15 _____ good   16-20 _____ great

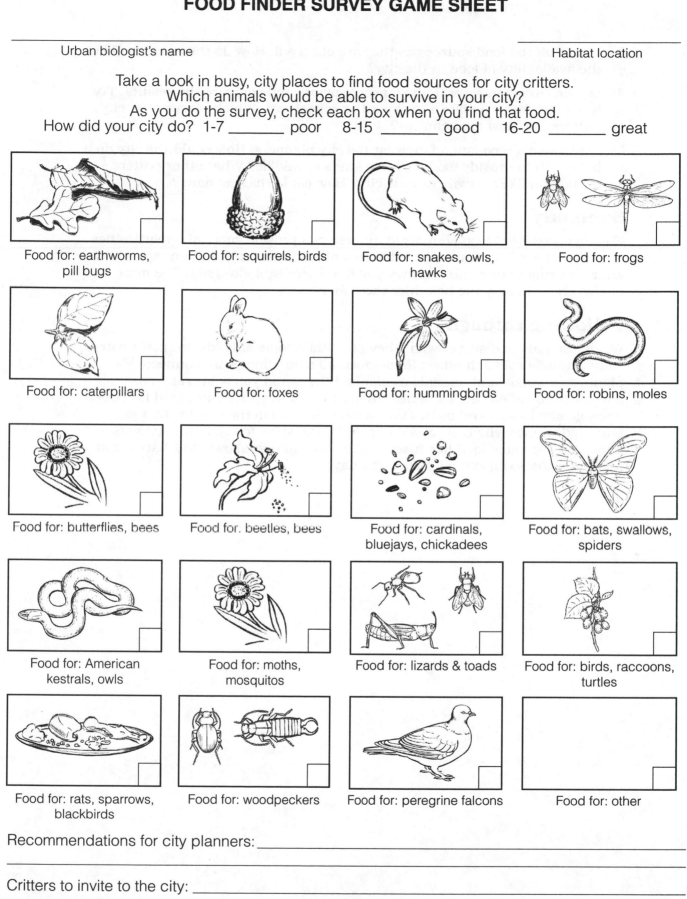

Food for: earthworms, pill bugs

Food for: squirrels, birds

Food for: snakes, owls, hawks

Food for: frogs

Food for: caterpillars

Food for: foxes

Food for: hummingbirds

Food for: robins, moles

Food for: butterflies, bees

Food for: beetles, bees

Food for: cardinals, bluejays, chickadees

Food for: bats, swallows, spiders

Food for: American kestrals, owls

Food for: moths, mosquitos

Food for: lizards & toads

Food for: birds, raccoons, turtles

Food for: rats, sparrows, blackbirds

Food for: woodpeckers

Food for: peregrine falcons

Food for: other

Recommendations for city planners:_____
_____

Critters to invite to the city: _____
_____

Plan of action: _____
_____

3. Check off the food sources as they are observed. How do the seasons affect the availability of food in the city?

4. Do the survey in several busy, people places and compare the results. Try it in other habitats like a backyard or schoolyard. Which places offer city critters the most food choices?

5. Now make a recommendation for the city planners. How could the city do a better job to provide food for more kinds of wildlife? What other critters would you like to invite to your city? How could that get done?

Summary

Having a variety of food sources in an area can provide survival opportunities to a greater variety of animals. When scientists find many different species of animals living in one habitat, they say that there is biodiversity. The more biodiversity, usually the healthier the habitat.

Following through

Watch animals to discover what they eat. While some animals are plant-eaters, some animals eat each other! Remember, all living things are connected—plants to animals and animals to plants. Why would you want rats, snakes, and other so-called "undesirables" to live in your city? They are food for larger animals like hawks and owls. Draw a food chain from the habitat that was surveyed. Notice which species compete for the same foods. Some animals might eat the same food like insect-eating bats and swallows, but bats eat at night and the swallows eat during the day.

Critter congregations

Subjects

Science, math, social studies.

Concepts

Science skills

Observing, predicting, recording.

Focus

Life in the city can be easier than in the wild for some animals because there are fewer large predators. But by instinct, animals use behaviors that help them escape from being a meal, even in the city. What city critters gather in large numbers to avoid predators?

Did you know?

A pair of robins usually has two broods of four birds each during the breeding season. In 10 years, if all the birds survived, the offspring of this one pair of robins would total 19,500,000 birds! That many birds would soon eat all the available food, and many would starve. But predators, disease, and severe weather all work to control the number of birds. The healthiest and most alert birds are the ones that survive to build nests and have babies. In this way, predators help keep the balance in nature. Robins often travel and feed in flocks, which lessens their chances of attack by predators.

Robin

What you need

❑ Critter Congregation Tally Sheet
❑ Pencil
❑ Binoculars (optional)

Before you start

❑ An ornithologist is an expert in the study of birds.

What you do

1. Ornithologists—while walking or driving through the city, look for bird "meeting places." Some places where birds might gather in large numbers are parking lots, shopping malls, city parks, courtyards of office buildings, dumpsters, groves of trees, landfills, and water treatment facilities.

CRITTER CONGREGATION TALLY SHEET

Estimate the number of birds
seen at different meeting places.
Make notes about the birds' behavior.

Ornithologist's name _____

Date _____

MEETING PLACE	sparrows	starlings	blackbirds	cedar waxwings	robins	seagulls
shopping mall						
building						
courtyard						
city park						
dumpster or landfill						
water treatment facility						
groves of trees						
other						

Notes: _____

_____

2. Observe the birds' behavior when they are in these meeting places. What are they doing? How do they interact with each other? Do they get along or fight? How close do they get to one another? Do they make noises? If so, what kind?

3. Try to guess how many birds are meeting there. Imagine a "block of birds." Count the number of birds in the block. How many more of the blocks would the flock contain? The number of birds in the block times the number of blocks gives an estimated count of birds.

4. When are critter congregations usually seen? Can this behavior be observed year-round, or is it seasonal?

5. Watch for an interesting behavior called "mobbing." When a predator such as a fox, dog, house cat, hawk, or owl is discovered, a bird will sound out its alarm call. Birds of many different species will come and join together to chase the predator from the area by diving and squawking at it.

Summary

Flocking or grouping together in large numbers is one type of animal survival strategy that can be easily observed in the city. Some birds roost together for the night in these city places or use the area for feeding. In flocks, birds gain protection from predators like hawks, owls, house cats, and raccoons. Often birds are following their food supply. Many species of birds flock together just before and during migration.

Following through

Does your city welcome crowds of critters? People sometimes complain about the nuisance caused by perching birds who splatter cars in parking lots. Parkgoers get grouchy about park benches covered with droppings. In your opinion, what should people do about critter congregations in cities?

Wildlife at work

Concepts

Science skills

Observing, predicting, recording.

Focus

All living things have a job in the community where they live. Even in "unused" places, wildlife is at work. When people change the use of a piece of land, often the balance of nature is disturbed. What can we learn about yielding to animal and plant communities so they can live and work?

Did you know?

Without a cleanup crew of slugs, beetles, worms, and ants, there would be a big pile of dead dinosaurs downtown! Forests would be buried in fallen leaves. Without insect-eating bats and birds, the air would be swarming with pests. Many beneficial critters can share city spaces when we keep healthy habitats available. Helping wildlife helps people, too.

What you need

❑ Ribbon as survey markers
❑ Popsicle sticks
❑ Tape
❑ Yarn or rubber bands
❑ Pencils
❑ Scissors
❑ Wildlife at Work Community Survey Sheet

Before you start

❑ Make copies of the wildlife at work community survey sheet on yellow paper.
❑ Discuss some of the jobs that living things do. Examples are:
  • Pest controllers—praying mantis, ladybugs, spiders, and snakes
  • Cleanup crew—snail, slug, earthworm, flies, fungi, beetles, ants, vultures, crows
  • Food producers—plants
  • Soil conditioners—earthworms, fungi, decaying plants
  • Oxygen producers—plants
  • Population controllers—animals that eat other animals
  • Pollinators—bees, hummingbirds, butterflies, moths, beetles
  • Leaf eaters—sowbugs, caterpillars
  • Mosquito eaters—fish, dragonflies

WILDLIFE AT WORK COMMUNITY SURVEY SHEET

Cut out the YIELD signs and tape to sticks or thread with yarn.
Use the YIELD signs to record the living things and their jobs within the survey area outside.
Put the signs in places where the wildlife is at work.

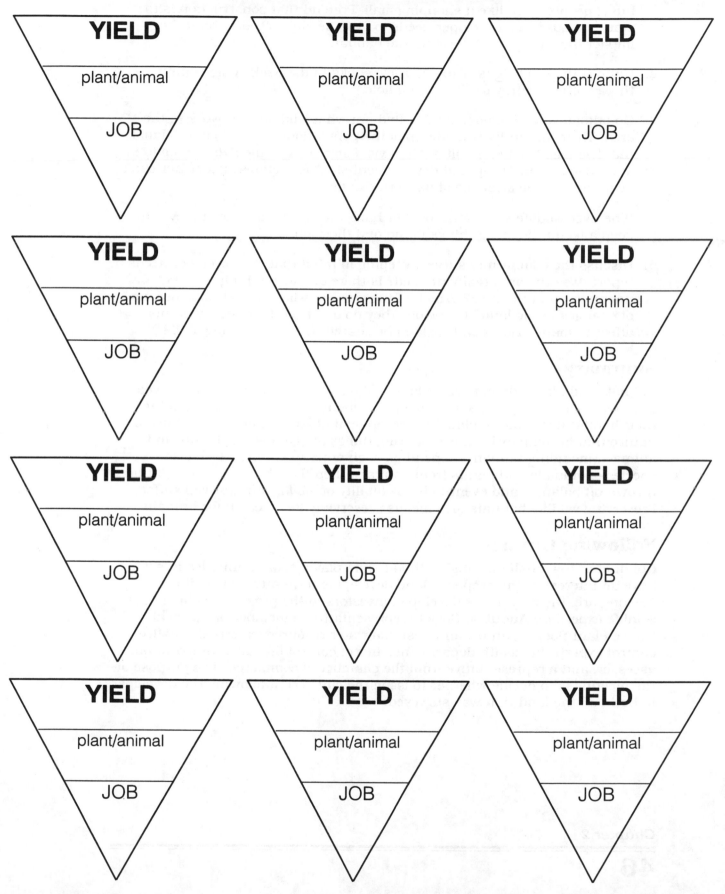

What you do

1. With surveyor ribbons, mark an "unused" area that is to be changed into a busy, people place like a shopping mall. Pretend that construction is to start soon, but the developer needs to give the city a report about the impact the changes will have on the habitat.

2. Cut out the yield signs. Tape popsicle sticks to the back of signs and thread others with yarn through a hole.

3. Go outside and challenge kids to find out what wildlife is at work in the area. The community is made up of the populations of plants and animals that live together in a habitat. On a yield sign, record the living thing found and its job in the "proposed development site." Remember, if a critter can't be found, maybe evidence of its work can be.

4. Wherever wildlife is at work, post or hang the signs. Ask one surveyor to keep a list of the living things found and their jobs.

5. Discuss the community survey, keeping in mind that the developer needs a report. Was the area really unused? Is there any living thing that is unemployed in the area? Which of the workers will lose their jobs because of changes to the land? If the jobs they do don't get done, how will this affect humans? How can this land be shared by humans and wildlife?

Summary

Animals and plants do important jobs that also benefit humans. Some even have more than one job! As we learn more about their jobs, we can yield to their habitat needs as we plan for development of land. There is a balance in nature that is complex because all living things are connected. Plants and animals, including humans, depend on each other to survive. If we lose species of animals and plants from habitats, then the whole system might be thrown off balance, and eventually the quality of life for humans will suffer. Preserving wildlife habitats also means preserving life on earth for humans.

Following through

Conduct a "town hall meeting" with kids role-playing community leaders who have an interest in the proposed land development. In attendance at the meeting are: the mayor, the developer, investors in the project, neighbors, a wildlife expert, an Audubon Society representative, a member of the local Native Plant Society, an urban forester, a water resource expert, air quality control expert, the health department's insect control manager, the local tax assessor, and a representative from the chamber of commerce. The purpose of the meeting is to decide whether to issue the city permit allowing the developer to build on the land that was surveyed.

Suggested books

Bash, Barbara. 1990. *Urban Roosts*. New York: Sierra Club Books.

> This colorful picture book was written for children, but it is a wonderful source of background information about common urban birds.

Dowden, Anne Ophelia. 1994. *Poisons in Our Path.* New York: Harper Collins.

> This book will make sure that you recognize plants such as poison ivy, and it will also teach you how important various poisonous plants are to the environment.

Dowden, Anne Ophelia. 1972. *Wild Green Things in the City*. New York: Thomas Y. Crowell.

> The beautiful and accurate paintings of wild plants in this book will inspire appreciation of even the simplest weed.

Garber, Steven D. 1987. *The Urban Naturalist*. New York: John Wiley & Sons.

> An inspiring collection of natural history essays about urban ecology.

Herberman, Ethan. 1989. *The City Kids' Field Guide.* New York: Simon & Schuster.

> A wonderful source of information for adults who inspire kids to see nature around them. Herberman explains how dozens of species have learned to survive in city places.

Lauber, Patricia. 1986. *From Flower to Flower, Animals and Pollination.* New York: Crown Publishers.

> Remarkable photographs and stimulating text explain how flowers and their animal pollinators come together in a way that mutually benefits each other.

Martin, Alexander, Zim, Herbert and Arnold Nelson. 1961. *American Wildlife & Plants*. New York: Dover Publications, Inc.

> This is the authoritative guide to the eating habits of wildlife.

Pringle, Lawrence. 1977. *Animals and Their Niches*. New York: William Morrow & Co.

> Pringle has explained a complex ecological concept by describing the niches of several common animals.

Discovering critters in great green spaces 3

Investigate vacant lots, unmowed areas, parks, golf courses, ball fields, and open fields to see what animals take advantage of these city habitats. As wild land has been turned into manicured recreational areas for people, some animals still find that these habitats suit their needs. Ducks and geese swim in golf course waterways, and bats and birds eat beetles and moths attracted to bright ball-field lights. The killdeer plover, a bird that naturally nests on the ground at the edge of a meadow or marshy mud flat, is often seen nesting on ball fields, golf courses, or the edge of parking lots.

Some of the great green spaces in a city might be more "natural" than others. If you're lucky, you might have an urban forest nearby. How are the parks in your city maintained? Often parks are mowed and pruned so that natural layers of vegetation are removed, leaving a flat, green lawn with large trees towering above. Animals that use the middle, shrubbery layer are not invited! Investigating the wildness of these city green spaces can be a good study in biodiversity. Some of the activities from chapter 5, "Exploring backyards and schoolyards," can also be done in great green spaces.

Remember urban explorer manners; be sure to have permission before entering someone else's property. Also, leave animals in their homes and learn through observation. When animals are collected for temporary study, they can be observed, drawn, or photographed and then returned to their habitats. Remember not to impact the delicate balance of nature while exploring great green spaces.

Habitat hunt

Subjects

Science, social studies, language arts.

Skills

Observing, recording, predicting.

Focus

Animals need certain habitats to survive. That's the place they are best suited to find food, water, shelter, and space to raise their young. What critters will you discover in the great green spaces in or near your city?

Did you know?

Fireflies have glowing glands at the tip of their body that flash lights in the night to signal and attract mates. These beetles were once common in damp, grassy habitats east of the Rocky Mountains, where their developing larvae could live underground and hunt for snails, slugs, and worms. The widespread use of DDT, a chemical pesticide, almost wiped them out. Now that DDT has been banned and their habitats are healthier, fireflies are gaining in numbers again. Watch with wonder as these magical insects flicker in the summer night over meadows and lawns.

Firefly

What you need

❑ Habitat Hunt Activity Sheet
❑ Pencil
❑ Binoculars (optional)

What you do

1. Using the Habitat Hunt Activity Sheet, have urban explorers discover critters in parks, golf courses, ball fields, playgrounds, or vacant lots and open fields.

2. Look for animal hideouts and hangouts like perches, nest sites, feeding places, and wet spots.

3. Circle or check the critters observed in the great green space. On the Habitat Hunt Activity Sheet, draw or note any other animals discovered and where they were seen. What was the best time to see the animals?

4. On the back of the activity sheet, list green spaces your city offers to animals and people.

HABITAT HUNT ACTIVITY SHEET

Urban explorer's name _____

Date _____

Explore a great green space and look for these critters.
Draw or note any other living things you discover and where you found them.

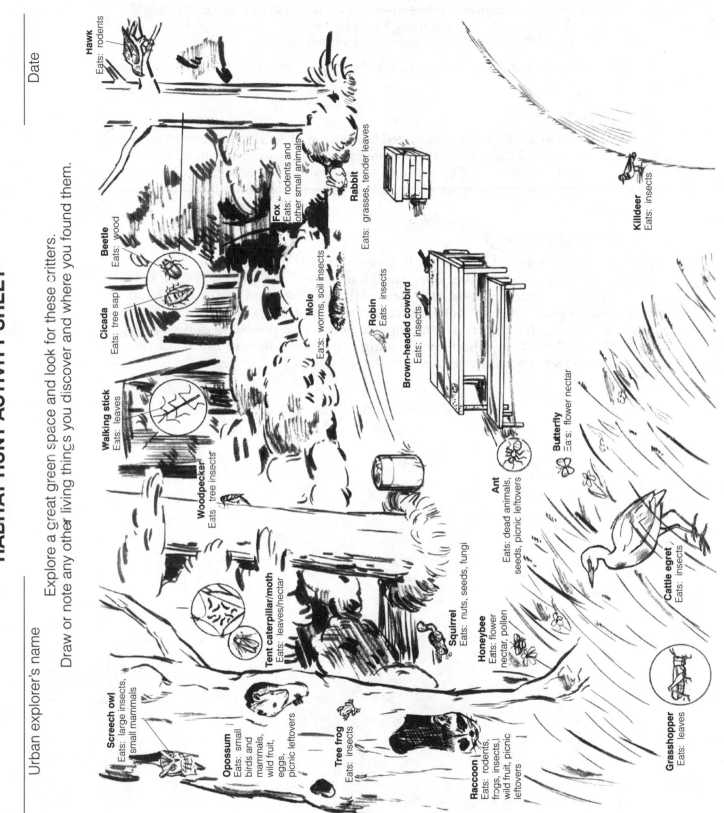

Hawk
Eats: rodents

Beetle
Eats: wood

Cicada
Eats: tree sap

Walking stick
Eats: leaves

Woodpecker
Eats: tree insects

Fox
Eats: rodents and other small animals

Rabbit
Eats: grasses, tender leaves

Mole
Eats: worms, soil insects

Robin
Eats: insects

Brown-headed cowbird
Eats: insects

Killdeer
Eats: insects

Screech owl
Eats: large insects, small mammals

Opossum
Eats: small birds and mammals, wild fruit, eggs, picnic leftovers

Tent caterpillar/moth
Eats: leaves/nectar

Tree frog
Eats: insects

Squirrel
Eats: nuts, seeds, fungi

Raccoon
Eats: rodents, frogs, insects, wild fruit, picnic leftovers

Honeybee
Eats: flower nectar, pollen

Ant
Eats: dead animals, seeds, picnic leftovers

Butterfly
Eats: flower nectar

Cattle egret
Eats: insects

Grasshopper
Eats: leaves

5. How could your city offer more green space habitat? What if some areas in parks were left unmowed? What animals would be attracted to the city if some dead trees were left standing? Is land beside roadways seeded with wildflowers? What if buildings were landscaped with native plants?

6. What threats and dangers do animals face in the great green spaces of the city?

Summary

As more and more wild land is changed into city spaces, it is important to save green spaces for wildlife. Great green spaces, both large and small, whether in the city or in the country, offer habitats to many animals. Keeping habitats healthy, clean, and free of toxic chemicals is the responsibility of all citizens—young and old.

Following through

Write to the chamber of commerce to find out if your city has "ecotourism." Wildlife viewing is the number one outdoor activity in the United States. Do people travel to watch wildlife in or near your city? What natural habitats do they visit? Nature tourism includes all activities that get people outdoors, like hunting, fishing, hiking, rock-climbing, canoeing, bird-watching and camping. Create a brochure that describes the natural treasures in your area and invites visitors to come and appreciate the wildlife in your city.

GREAT GREENERY SURVEY SHEET

Great greenery survey

Subjects

Science, math.

Concepts

Science skills

Comparing and contrasting, classifying, cause and effect.

Focus

Since food chains begin with plants, a variety of greenery is important for a diverse habitat. Naturally occurring plants grow in many layers, which allows different animal species to pick the place where they are best suited for survival. What plants make up the great green spaces in your city?

Did you know?

In growing cities, often trees are just "in the way" of where a house or store will be built. For every four urban trees that are cut down, only one is replanted. Some cities now have urban foresters whose job is to help the city and individuals plan for the wise use of land and the conservation of trees and other native plants.

What you need

❑ Pencil
❑ Ribbons or string for boundary markers
❑ Great Greenery Survey Sheet

What you do

1. Divide kids into survey groups. Choose two different types of great green spaces for this comparison survey. For example, in a city park survey the picnic area and the wooded park edge.

2. Mark off an area about 12' × 12' in the great greenery survey space using ribbons or string. Use the same size area for surveying both green space 1 and 2.

3. Record the variety of plants on the survey sheet.

4. Look for plants forming different height layers. What animals can be observed in the different layers?

Summary

Some green spaces in the city are more natural than others. An open field or vacant lot offers more habitat possibilities for wildlife than a mowed golf course fairway. A diversity of plant life supports a diverse and healthy wildlife

Great greenery survey

GREAT GREENERY SURVEY SHEET

_____   _____
Botanist's name   Date

Choose 2 different kinds of green spaces to explore.
Record the kinds and numbers of plants within the survey area.

PLANT TYPE	GREEN SPACE 1:	GREEN SPACE 2:
trees		
shrubs		
vines		
grasses		
herbs (wildflowers)		

1. Which great green space has more varieties of plants? _____

2. What plants form these layers?   <u>CANOPY</u>   <u>SHRUB</u>   <u>GROUND</u>

green space 1: _____

_____

green space 2: _____

_____

3. What critters did you see?   <u>CANOPY</u>   <u>SHRUB</u>   <u>GROUND</u>

green space 1: _____

_____

green space 2: _____

_____

Canopy

Understory

Shrub layer

Ground

population. Different species of wildlife, especially birds, live at different heights in the plant layers. Missing plant layers mean missing species.

Following through

See plant diversity activity in chapter 5, "Food factory." Experiment with an area of green space at school or in your backyard. It's easy—just don't do anything. Leave an area unmowed. Then watch and see what plants move in and take over. Make a journal and check every two weeks to record the observations about plant and animal life in the area as new plants grow and change the landscape.

Have older students research native plants and compile a list of suggestions for their area. Write to city leaders to promote landscaping for wildlife in city parks and around buildings. Include a copy of the survey results to support their ideas.

Micro/macro-hike

Subjects
Science, art.

Concepts

Science skills
Observing, describing, classifying.

Focus
Every living thing has a role to play in its community. Some make food (producers), while some eat food (consumers). Decomposers feed on dead plants and animals and break them down into simpler nutrients, which recycle to the soil. What producers, consumers, and decomposers can you discover in a great green space? What evidence of interactions can you find among living things?

Did you know?
The housefly is a scavenger—hunting for rotting garbage, dead plants, and animals to eat. The fly spits on its food and then soaks up dissolved nutrients with its spongelike mouthpiece. The rotting organic matter is not only a restaurant for flies, but also a nursery where the fly lays its eggs. The eggs hatch into larvae (maggots) that recycle the nutrients of the dead organisms as they feed on the decaying matter. Houseflies are thought of as disease-carrying pests, but they perform an important role as a decomposer in nature.

Housefly on garbage

What you need
For each pair:
❑ Hand lens
❑ 18" length of string
❑ Micro/Macro-Hike Activity Sheets
❑ Pencil

Before you start
❑ Practice using a hand lens by holding it 1 inch from an object. While looking through the lens, move it slowly away from the object towards one eye until it is magnified and clearly focused.
❑ Review these word meanings: produce—make, producer—food maker, consume—eat, consumer—eater, decompose—rot, decomposer—soil maker.

MICRO-HIKE ACTIVITY SHEET

_____   _____
Nature detective's name   Habitat

Using a hand lens, investigate the micro-habitat along your string trail.
Draw or list the discoveries in these spaces.

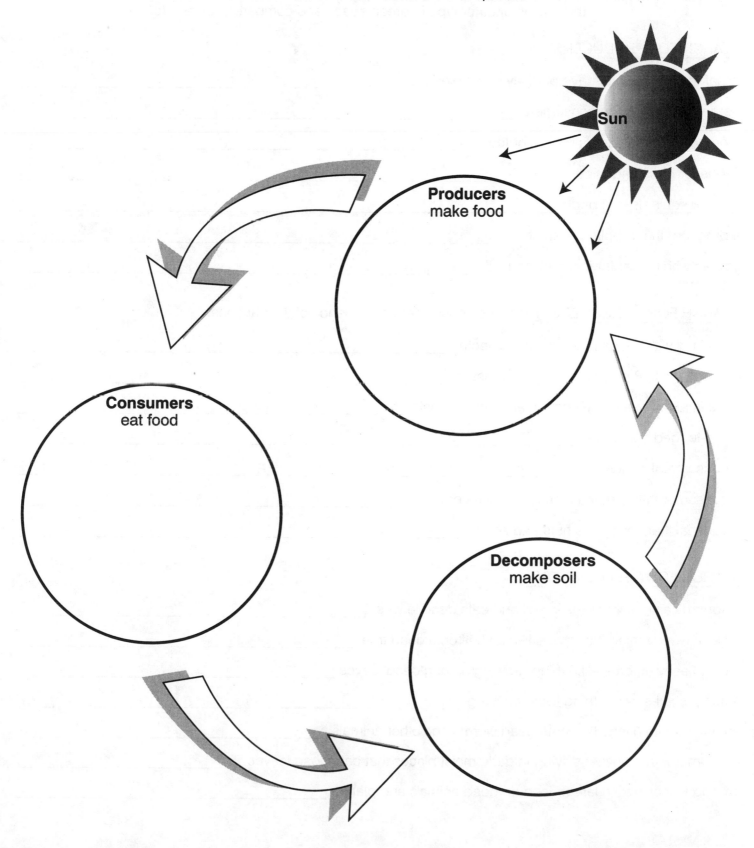

Sun

Producers
make food

Consumers
eat food

Decomposers
make soil

MACRO-HIKE ACTIVITY SHEET

_____   _____
Nature detective's name   Habitat

Take a hike in a great green space to discover producers, consumers, and decomposers.
Look for evidence of interactions between living things. Record your observations.
Try this hike in another type of green space and compare your results.

SEARCH FOR PRODUCERS:

a leaf that caterpillars have partially consumed _____

berries that birds can consume _____

a producer that squirrels have nibbled _____

seeds for birds and mice _____

nuts for squirrels and birds _____

a producer that rabbits consume _____

flowers with nectar for insects and birds _____

SEARCH FOR CONSUMERS: Find these consumers or evidence of their actions.

an animal with 6 legs that consumes nectar _____

an animal with 8 legs that consumes insects _____

an animal that consumes both plants and animals _____

a two-legged consumer _____

a consumer that hunts _____

a consumer that is eaten by other consumers _____

an animal that consumes nuts and seeds _____

SEARCH FOR DECOMPOSERS:

a squirmy animal that lives in soil and eats dead leaves _____

a hard, woody thing that grows like a shelf on a dead tree _____

a soft, fleshy umbrella-like thing growing among dead leaves _____

a fuzzy, shell-shaped thing living on a log _____

an animal with 6 legs that eats dead worms and other animals _____

an animal with many legs living in dark, moist places that eats dead leaves _____

a flying insect whose larvae feed on dead animals and plants _____

What you do

Micro-hike

1. Pair up with a hiking partner and choose an interesting piece of ground in a great green space.

2. Lay out the length of string to make a miniature trail and begin the "hike." Investigate the micro-habitat with a hand lens.

3. Draw or list the discoveries in the boxes on the Micro-Hike Activity Sheet.

4. Give a guided tour of the string trail to another team of "hikers."

Macro-hike

1. Using the Macro-hike Activity Sheet, nature detectives go outside and explore great green spaces.

2. Search for producers, consumers, and decomposers and record your observations.

Kids on a micro-hike

Summary

Interactions among living things are not always obvious, but even in a small space, a closer look reveals producers, consumers, and decomposers busy at work. The cycle of life is fueled by the energy of the sun. When plants and animals die, their nutrients return to the earth and enrich the soil, which nourishes new growing plants, and the cycle continues.

Insect investigations

Subject

Science.

Concepts

Science skills

Observing, describing, classifying.

Focus

There are more insects in the city than any other type of critter. They are easy-to-find examples of animal adaptation to habitat. Because of their adaptations, insects are often found in very specific places within their habitat. What insects can you find buzzing, crawling, hopping, or flying in great green spaces near you?

Did you know?

Insects are found just about everywhere, but some might be hard to see because they are camouflaged. The oleander moth has a color pattern that blends in with the bark of a tree where it rests during the day. Its coloration makes it hard for daytime predators to see it. Camouflage can also help predators hide. The shape and color of the praying mantis allows it to blend in with greenery while waiting to snatch an insect that flies by. Habitat adaptations like these give insects a survival advantage.

Praying mantis with its prey

What you need

For each person:
- ❑ 2 clear plastic cups (8-oz. size)
- ❑ Scissors
- ❑ Mesh or netting
- ❑ A rubber band
- ❑ Pencil
- ❑ Insect Investigations Activity Sheet
- ❑ White sheets (can be shared)
- ❑ White plastic tubs (can be shared)

Before you start

- ❑ An entomologist studies insects. All adult insects have: six legs, three body parts (head, thorax, abdomen), two antennae, and most have one or two pairs of wings.
- ❑ Be careful when handling insects. Some bite or sting to defend themselves.
- ❑ Many insects are fragile; take care not to damage legs, wings, or antennae.

Chapter 3

INSECT INVESTIGATIONS ACTIVITY SHEET

Entomologist's name _____

Date _____

Where are these types of insects found?
How many did you find in each place?

INSECT TYPE	Total Number Seen	on trees or shrubs	on flowers, grass, weeds	in or on the ground	in the air	Survival Strategy
						can lie flat in small spaces; nocturnal, eats variety of decaying matter
						camouflaged by shape and color, can fly or hop
						can fly, some are small, some camouflaged by color, found in many different habitats
						jump and fly, camouflaged by color, found on many different plants
						camouflaged by color and shape, can fly
						hide in cracks and crevices, scavenges for food, stings for defense
						breed in city ponds, sewers, ditches and standing water in man-made containers, strong fliers
						eat people's garbage, can fly, good eyesight, quick movement, some mimic bees or wasps
						can fly, sting for defense, some live in social groups
						can fly, adults eat a variety of foods, some feed on fermented material found in urban garbage

What you do

1. To make an insect observation chamber, cut the bottom two-thirds off one of the plastic cups. Cut a mesh circle and rubber band it in place over the top of the cut cup. Trim any extra mesh off. Slip the cut cup into the other cup to form the top of the chamber. The mesh-covered top lifts off easily as entomologists bring the two chamber pieces back together around an insect.

2. To collect insects from a bush or small tree, place a sheet on the ground. Shake the plant. As insects fall into the sheet, grab the four corners and lift up to gather the insects in the middle of the sheet. Carefully release the insects into a plastic tub with a mesh or clear top that will allow observation.

3. Take the collection materials and go look for insects in great green spaces. Some might be observed without collecting. Collect some for temporary study. Using the Insect Investigations Activity Sheet, record the findings and look for urban survival strategies.

4. Return all the insects to their habitats.

5. Try the activity in different types of city green spaces and compare the results. How does plant diversity in the different areas affect the insect investigations? Which places have more insects? Which has a greater variety of insects? What insects can you now predict will be found in certain places within a habitat?

Summary

It is possible to find out a lot about an insect and the type of habitat it needs by observing where it lives and how it moves. It's not necessary to know its name. Most insects are found on or near their food source. Some butterflies feed on rotting fruits and vegetables that are easy to find in the city. A monarch butterfly sips nectar from a variety of wildflowers, but it will only lay its eggs on the milkweed plant. The milkweed is the "host plant" for munching monarch larvae. The toxic substances absorbed from the milkweed into the caterpillar's body make the monarchs taste bad to predators. The butterflies will return to the same area each year in search of host plants. A great green space with a wide variety of plants attracts higher numbers of different kinds of insects.

Following through

Explore a fallen tree or rotten log to see what insects have adapted to live in that microhabitat. Lift a rock and check out the hidden insect community. Be careful—snakes, spiders, scorpions, or other animals that can bite or sting might live there, too. Always put the rock or log back where it was. Can you think of reasons why?

Soil sampler

Subjects
Science, math.

Science skills
Observing, classifying, comparing, and contrasting.

Focus
Soil makes up the outermost layer of our planet. It is formed by rocks and decaying plants and animals. Plants depend on soil to grow. A hidden world of animals lives in the soil. What critters will you unearth when you dig up a square-foot soil sample in a great green space?

Did you know?
Five to ten tons of animal life can live in an acre of soil. An acre is 43,560 square feet of land, which is about the size of a football field. Earthworms and other decomposers digest fallen leaves and dead plants and make the surface soil richer. One earthworm can digest 36 tons of soil in one year! (That much soil weighs as much as 36 pickup trucks.) Fungi and bacteria also break down organic matter in the soil. Mice take seeds and plant materials into underground burrows, where the materials decay and become part of the soil. The burrows of ground-dwelling mammals such as moles and shrews allow oxygen into the soil, which benefits other critters living in the soil.

What you need
For each pair:
- ❑ A pencil and 12" ruler
- ❑ Soil Sampler Critter I.D. Sheet
- ❑ Shovel or hand trowel
- ❑ Hand lens
- ❑ 2 shoe boxes
- ❑ Spoon
- ❑ Damp paper towel

Before you start
- ❑ Some soil critters will bite or sting to defend themselves. Be cautious of centipedes, ants, and spiders.

SOIL SAMPLER CRITTER I.D. SHEET

Soil scientist's name

Habitat

Look for a variety of insects and noninsects in the square foot soil sample.
Identify the critters and record the number found.

Number of legs	Critter Type		How many found?
28 or more	millipede		
	centipede		
12 to 14	sow bug		
8	spider		
	mite		
	scorpion		
	daddy long-leg		
6	scarab beetle		
	bristletail		
	earwig		
	termite		
	ant		
	springtail		
	ground beetle larva		
	wireworm		
	tiger beetle larva		
	May beetle larva		
4	mole, toad		
no legs	earthworm		
	slug, snail		

What you do

1. Have the soil scientists pick partners and go outside to choose an interesting place to dig. Then measure and mark off a 12-inch square on the ground.

2. Partners take turns digging. Shovel soil into one of the shoe boxes. Shake and sift it to sort out critters.

3. Place the damp paper towel in the bottom of the other box. With a spoon, lift out any soil critters from the sorting box and place them in the prepared shoe box. Keep a lid on the box since most soil animals are sensitive to light and can also dry out easily. Check the moisture in the soil. Is it dry? Moist? Wet?

4. Dump soil from the sorting box next to the hole. Keep digging and sifting until the soil sample hole is 12 inches deep. What depth were most critters found? Surface? Midlevel? Lower?

5. Using the Soil Sampler Critter I.D. Sheet, sort and identify the animals.

6. Return the soil critters to the soil pile and gently push the soil back into the hole.

7. Try sampling the soil in different green spaces. How do the results compare from a mowed lawn and an area littered with fallen leaves? Which soil provides the richest habitat? How did the soil moisture content seem to affect the presence of soil critters?

Summary

Even though soil is not alive, there is a lot of life in it. Many critters have adapted to life underground where it's cool, dark, and damp. By eating and working there in the soil, they recycle nutrients from dead animals and plants into the soil. This enriched soil is used by growing plants, which then become food for animals. The cycle of life is rooted in the soil.

Following through

Spoon some of the soil sample into a small clay pot or plastic cup. Water it and put it in a sunny window. Check for signs of plant growth to see if there were any seeds in the soil that was investigated.

Bury lunch leftovers—from plastic bags to banana peels—to check for decomposition rates of the different items. Check once a week and keep a journal of the soil-making process.

Suggested books

Eyewitness Visual Dictionary Series. 1992 *The Visual Dictionary of Plants.* Dorling Kindersley, Inc.

> This pictorial dictionary provides everything you need to know about plants.

Imes, Rick. 1990. *The Practical Botanist.* New York: Simon & Schuster.

> A wealth of background information about plants as well as a good resource for activities to do with children to reinforce their understanding of plants. The chapter on "Urban Botany" is particularly relevant.

Imes, Rick. 1990. *The Practical Entomologist.* New York: Simon & Schuster.

> This is a really good guide to observing and understanding the world of insects.

Lauber, Patricia. *Seeds: Pop, Stick Slide,* New York: Crown Publishers, Inc., 1981.

> With its marvelous photographs and text, this book explains how seeds travel.

Milne, Lorus and Margery. *A Shovelful of Earth*, New York: Holt & Co. 1987.

> Read this book to learn about the kinds of creatures you might find in your soil survey; shows how to examine soil dwellers more closely with simple experiments.

Parker, Nancy Winslow. *Bugs.* 1987. New York: Greenwillow Books.

> A colorful and easy-to-read book that gives fun, yet complete and accurate, explanations.

Shepherd, Elizabeth. 1988. *No Bones: A Key to Bugs and Slugs, Worms and Ticks, Spiders and Centipedes.* New York: Macmillan Publishing Company.

> A wonderful resource for city kids to learn how to identify small urban wildlife.

Suziki, David and Barbara Hehner. 1986. *Looking at Insects.* New York: John Wiley & Sons.

> This book is a wealth of information and activities related to the study of insects.

Pondering ponds & other wonderful wet places

4

Ponds, puddles, ditches, bayous, streams, rivers, marshes, lakes, bays, and oceans are all wonderful wet places. The activities in this chapter focus on freshwater environments and the communities of life that depend on them. Urban explorers will discover that some animals are full-time residents, and others depend on watery habitats to complete a part of their life cycle. Some critters might come to the water's edge just for a drink. Plant and animal relationships can be easily observed within a pond because the habitat boundaries are well defined by the water itself.

Plan ahead for safety when exploring wonderful wet places. Some suggested guidelines include having children:
1. Use a buddy system.
2. Stay near adult leaders.
3. Wear closed-toe shoes.
4. Only put their hands in places where they can see.
5. When possible, lie on the stomach while looking into water to keep from falling in!

Try to have an adult leader for every five children.

Habitats and wildlife need to be protected, too. Don't trample the edges of wonderful wet places or disturb nests of turtles that might be hidden there. Certain sites might call for additional rules to be set by the adult leaders. To return aquatic specimens to their habitats safely, lower the container into the water, tilt it, and let the animal swim out.

By gathering evidence of the interdependent community of living things that exist in a wonderful wet place, children will learn the importance of keeping water clean to support the abundant plant and animal life they find. Everyone should get wet and muddy and have fun in the process!

Pondering ponds & other wonderful wet places

Habitat hunt

Subject
Science.

Concepts

Science skills
Observing, recording.

Focus
Since water is necessary for living things, wet places naturally attract wild animals. Both air-breathing and water-breathing animals make use of water habitats where they can find food, shelter, and a place to raise their young. What critters will you observe in or near a city pond?

Did you know?
Some animals live on land or in the air but depend on an aquatic habitat as a place to raise their young. Dragonflies and damselflies lay eggs on the water's surface. Damselflies cut holes in submerged plant stems and lay their eggs inside. The eggs hatch and become larvae. The damselfly and dragonfly's larval stage, called a nymph, burrows into the muck at the bottom of slow-moving water. City ponds and drainage ditches are just the place! There the nymphs hunt aquatic insects, worms, small snails, and tadpoles. After the nymph grows, it climbs out of the water on a plant stem. After resting, its outer covering splits open and the adult insect emerges ready for life in the air. Different life stages need different types of habitats.

Dragonfly nymph

What you need
❏ Habitat Hunt Activity Sheet
❏ Pencil

Before you start
❏ Review safety rules before exploring near water. Use a buddy system.

What you do
1. Using the Habitat Hunt Activity Sheet, urban explorers look for plants and animals that make up a pond community. If possible, take a look at different ponds. What life is supported by a park pond with concrete sides as compared to a more naturally occurring pond? Why?

2. Encourage kids to approach a pond slowly and quietly. What birds or large animals are near the pond? What animals are in the open water area that might dive deeper as you get closer?

3. Circle or check the critters and plants observed at the pond site. On the Habitat Hunt Activity Sheet, draw or note any other living things discovered and where they were seen. What was the best time to see

HABITAT HUNT ACTIVITY SHEET

Urban explorer's name _____   Date _____

Check off the critters and plants observed in a pond community in your city.
Draw or note any other living things you discover and where you saw them in the wonderful wet place.

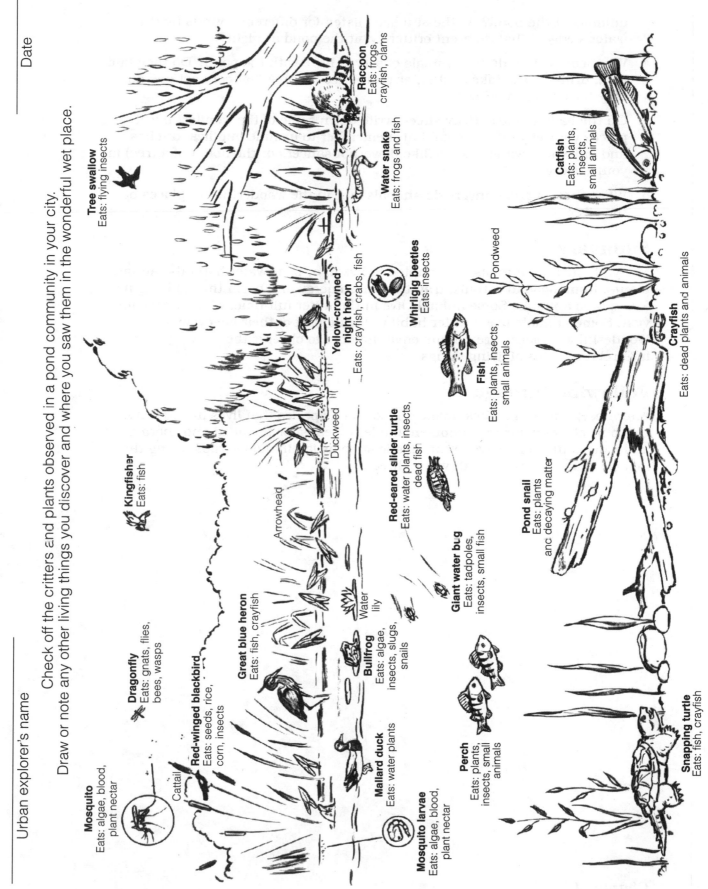

Mosquito
Eats: algae, blood, plant nectar

Dragonfly
Eats: gnats, flies, bees, wasps

Kingfisher
Eats: fish

Cattail

Red-winged blackbird
Eats: seeds, rice, corn, insects

Great blue heron
Eats: fish, crayfish

Mosquito larvae
Eats: algae, blood, plant nectar

Mallard duck
Eats: water plants

Perch
Eats: plants, insects, small animals

Bullfrog
Eats: algae, insects, slugs, snails

Water lily

Arrowhead

Giant water bug
Eats: tadpoles, insects, small fish

Duckweed

Yellow-crowned night heron
Eats: crayfish, crabs, fish

Red-eared slider turtle
Eats: water plants, insects, dead fish

Whirligig beetles
Eats: insects

Fish
Eats: plants, insects, small animals

Pondweed

Pond snail
Eats: plants and decaying matter

Crayfish
Eats: dead plants and animals

Snapping turtle
Eats: fish, crayfish

Tree swallow
Eats: flying insects

Raccoon
Eats: frogs, crayfish, clams

Water snake
Eats: frogs and fish

Catfish
Eats: plants, insects, small animals

animals at the pond? As the sun sets, listen for different sounds by the water's edge. What different critters visit the pond at night?

4. What connection do the animals observed have with the pond? Do they find food, drink water, take shelter, or reproduce there? What connections do they have to each other?

5. On the back of the activity sheet, write down some of the wonderful wet places your city offers as habitat. Remember to include puddles, ditches, and anywhere water stands (like flowerpot saucers or the notch of a tree) in your survey.

6. What threats and dangers do animals face in the wonderful wet places of the city?

Summary

Many plants and animals are adapted to live in or near water habitats. Aquatic plants, from algae to cattails, trap the sun's energy and begin the food chain for aquatic animals. Some animals live in the water full-time, while others just visit. Some animals use a water habitat during part of their life cycle. Wonderful wet places are unique environments to observe the interrelationships of living things.

Following through

After observing dragonflies, make a model of a species that lives in your city. Use pipe cleaners for the abdomen and legs, beads for the head and thorax, and wings cut from heavy, clear plastic such as lamination scraps. Hang the models from the ceiling with white thread.

Water sampler

Subject
Science.

Science skills
Observing, comparing and contrasting, recording.

Focus
Diversity of life is usually a sign of a healthy ecosystem. Physical factors like pH and water temperature affect water quality and biodiversity. Are the wonderful wet places in your city healthy?

Did you know?
The type of organisms found in a wonderful wet place can indicate its quality as a water habitat. Some animals and plants are more sensitive to factors in their environment than others. If larvae of blackflies and mayflies are found, water quality is good. When many tubiflex worms are found, the water is probably very low in oxygen. An overabundance of plants can actually be a sign of poor health for the wet place. Fertilizer runoffs from city lawns or country farms put too much nitrogen and phosphorus in the water. Plant life grows too fast and robs the water of oxygen as it dies and decays. Aquatic life suffers from this imbalance in nature.

Concepts

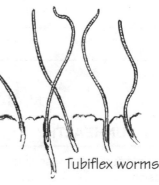

Tubiflex worms

Mayfly larvae

What you need
❑ Thermometer and string
❑ pH paper strips
❑ Empty plastic milk jugs
❑ Scissors and pencil
❑ White plastic tub
❑ Water Sampler Activity Sheet

Before you start
❑ Review safety rules for exploring near water.
❑ Make several water scoops from the milk jugs.

What you do
1. In various kinds of wonderful wet places, measure the physical characteristics of the water and take a look at the biodiversity. At each site, record the results on the Water Sampler Activity Sheet.

Cut away this piece

Water scoop made from milk jug

Water sampler

WATER SAMPLER ACTIVITY SHEET

_____   _____
Urban explorer's name   Date

Use this chart to find out if the wonderful wet places in your city are healthy.

Water habitat	PHYSICAL CHARACTERISTICS			BIOLOGICAL CHARACTERISTICS		OTHER	OVERALL HEALTH
	CLARITY/COLOR How far down into the water can you see? Does the water appear to have a color?	pH VALUE Is the water neutral, acid, or alkaline?	TEMP. What is the surface temp.? What is the bottom temp.?	PLANTS None visible? Plants along edges? Excess plants?	ANIMALS How many animal species did you see?	How have people changed this place?	Is the habitat healthy or is wildlife here in danger?
Habitat 1							
Habitat 2							
Habitat 3							

KEY TO HEALTHY/UNHEALTHY WATER CHARACTERISTICS

	UNHEALTHY	HEALTHY	UNHEALTHY
Clarity/Color	*Brown/cloudy color = sediment from erosion Yellow color = sulphur runoff from industrial site	Water that is clear allows sunlight to penetrate for the growth of plants and the production of food.	Green water indicates that too much fertilizer is coming from nearby fields causing excess algae.
pH Value	lemon juice/acid 1 — 2 — 3 — 4 frogs	rainwater neutral 5 — 6 — 7 — 8 — 9 large # of insect species snails, clams, mussels crustaceans bass, trout, crappie bacteria	ammonia/soaps 10 — 11 — 12 — 13 — 14
Temperature	28° — 38° Cooler temperatures slow growth of organisms.	48° — 55° — 68° — 78° trout, mayfly most plant life most bass, crappie, bluegill, caddis fly some plant life, salmon, trout, many insects	88° — 98° Warm water does not hold as much oxygen as cooler water. Water above 89° is in poor health.
Plants	No plants in the water means that there will be less food and oxygen for animal species.	Plant growth around the edges of pond/ditch, etc. provide food and cover for many animals.	Plants which cover the water can prevent the sunlight from penetrating.
Animals	The water is unhealthy if you find less than one or two species of animals.	The water habitat is healthy if you can see more than 6 kinds of animal species.	The water is unhealthy if 90% of the animals you find are made up of one kind of species.
People Influences	Excessive muddiness of water caused by building and development. Excessive algae or plant growth because of fertilizers draining into water.	Have people created projects to stop erosion, clean up litter, or planted native wetland plants where needed?	Oily sheen on the water caused by oil run-off from nearby roads. White foam (3" or more) caused by runoff of detergents or industrial chemicals.

*Brown sediment in water habitats with mud bottoms (as in Houston bayous) is not necessarily unhealthy.

After exploring the sites, contrast the kinds of life supported by the different types of wet places.

2. Use pH paper strips to find out if there are acids or alkalis dissolved in the various bodies of water. Dip the pH strip into the water being sampled. Compare the color of the dampened strip with the color chart on the side of paper dispenser.

3. Tie a length of string on the thermometer. Measure water temperature at the surface and then the bottom for one minute or more.

4. How does the water look? Is it clear or cloudy? Does the water have a color?

5. Make notes about the amount and type of plant life.

6. Survey the diversity of animal life at each site. With scoops, collect water from different places at the site to fill the white plastic tub. Count the number of different kinds of animals you can see.

7. Return the water samples and critters to the habitat.

Summary

Predictions of biodiversity in water habitats can be made from measurements of pH and water temperature. Most living things require a water pH between 5 and 9, but the largest variety of animals are adapted to live in water with a pH range of 6.5 to 7.5 (neutral). Temperature affects what can survive in the water because it impacts the rates of growth and decomposition in a body of water. Pollution decreases the quality of the habitat, which in turn lowers the diversity of life forms. Sometimes polluted waters actually support high numbers of organisms, but fewer kinds. Different types of living things are adapted to different types of water habitats. Just like the recipes in a cookbook, the ingredients of a habitat can be in differing amounts or arrangements as they are in the ponds, puddles, ditches, and streams studied. As a result, each site supports different kinds of animal and plant communities.

Following through

Find out about aquatic plants that can clean up water by filtering and absorbing pollutants.

Pond zone survey

Subjects
Science, art.

Concepts

Science skills
Observing, describing, classifying.

Focus
A pond is a small, shallow body of standing water made up of different microhabitats. What living things will you find on the surface, at the bottom, in the open water, and at the water's edge? As a nature detective, what can you discover about the adaptations of the aquatic animals you find?

Did you know?
The whirligig beetle swims in high-speed circles on the surface of the water. Since its back repels water but its lower surface does not, it floats half immersed. The beetle's divided eyes are well adapted for hunting other insects from this position. The upper part of each eye looks into the air while the lower part looks down into the water.

Whirligig beetle

This black, oval-shaped beetle whirls around on the surface breathing air until it is alarmed. Then it dives underwater and clings to a plant stem. To breathe underwater, it carries its air supply under its wings or in a bubble on its rear end!

What you need
- ❑ Several empty milk jugs
- ❑ 4 white plastic tubs
- ❑ Pencil and paper
- ❑ Wrigglers and Whirlers Observation Guide
- ❑ *A Field Guide to Pond Life*
- ❑ Hand lenses
- ❑ 2 clear plastic cups per person (8-oz. size)
- ❑ Mesh
- ❑ Fiberglass screen circles
- ❑ Rubber bands

Before you start
- ❑ Make water straining scoops from milk jugs.
- ❑ Make aquatic animal observation chambers (see chapter 3—Insect Investigations).
- ❑ Review rules for safety near water.

Cover with screening

Water strainer made from milk jug

Cut away this piece

❑ Make a pond zone survey chart by folding a piece of 8½"-x-11" paper in half and then in half again. Unfold it and label the four sections for each zone.

What you do

Activity 1

1. Investigate the four habitat zones using the collection methods described in the following. When specimens are collected, place them in water in white tubs in a cool, shady place. Use one tub for each different zone survey so specimens can be compared easily.

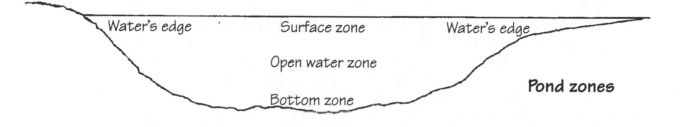

Water's edge   Surface zone   Water's edge

Open water zone

Pond zones

Bottom zone

Collection methods for pond zones:

- <u>Surface zone</u>—Scoop water from the top 1 to 2 inches of the pond's surface. The water's surface tension allows specially adapted animals to walk or glide right on top of the water. Other air-breathers live on the surface or just below it.

- <u>Water's edge zone</u>—Scoop water from the shallow area where plants are growing in the water. Where the land meets the water, there is a rich blend of concentrated resources for life. What interaction between plants and animals do you notice here?

- <u>Bottom zone</u>—Scoop up mud and plant debris from the bottom. As your scoop comes up through the water, you can collect specimens from other zones. Decomposition happens in the bottom zone. See who's at work cleaning up the rotting plants and dead animals of the pond. Does the mud smell? If so, that's evidence of microscopic bacteria at work.

- <u>Open water zone</u>—Observe it from a distance or attach the scoop to a long, strong pole for sampling. The center of the pond is used by large, free swimming animals like fish and turtles and microscopic plants and animals that drift in the water.

2. Take a closer look at specimens with a hand lens. Refer to *A Field Guide to Pond Life* to identify each catch. Replenish water in tubs as needed.

3. Record the findings on your pond zone survey chart.

4. Review the pond zone survey chart. Where were most of the pond organisms found? Why? What adaptations do the animals have to survive in the pond zones?

5. Have each person transfer one aquatic animal and some new water into the observation chamber for the next "pond zone" activity. Return the other specimens to the pond.

Activity 2

1. Take an "in-depth" look at aquatic animals using some of the catch from the pond zones. Use the Wrigglers and Whirlers Observation Guide to help discover the animals' adaptations to the water habitat.

2. Watch the animals' behavior and try to answer the questions on the Observation Guide. An overhead projector can be used to enlarge viewing of water specimens collected in a clear plastic shoe box.

3. Return the specimens to their habitat.

Summary

The most biodiversity will usually be found in the water's edge zone. Plants rooted in the pond bottom near the edge provide shelter and food sources for a wide variety of animals. Frogs, toads, tadpoles, small fish, insects, and their developing larvae have adapted to life in that habitat zone. Being able to breathe in a water environment is a requirement for aquatic animal survival. The animals observed show some amazing adaptations. The water strider insect breathes air and skates on the surface of the pond, while the whirligig beetle carries a bubble of air like an oxygen tank when it dives underwater. Mosquito larvae and water scorpions hang upside down under the surface and breathe through tubes. Fish, clams, crayfish, and dragonfly nymphs breathe through gills that take oxygen from the water.

Following through

Recreate the surveyed pond on a big window. Draw, color, and cut out the animals and plants that make up the pond community. Tape them on the window in the pond zone where they live.

WRIGGLERS AND WHIRLERS
An Aquatic Animal Observation Guide

_____
Urban explorer's name

_____
Date

Take an "in-depth" look at an individual specimen collected during the Pond Zone Survey.
Place one aquatic animal in the observation chamber and try to answer these questions.

1. What pond zone does the animal live in? _____

2. How long does it stay underwater? _____

3. Where does it rest? _____

Look for special features (adaptations) that improve the animal's chances for survival in that pond zone.

4. Describe how the animal moves: _____
_____

5. Does it have legs? _____ How many? _____ What kind? _____

6. If it does not have legs, what body parts does it use to get around? _____
_____

7. Is the animal an air-breather or water-breather? _____

8. How do you think it gets its air supply? _____

9. How do you think it gets its food? _____

10. What does it eat? _____

11. What does it do when it is alarmed? _____

12. Draw a picture of the specimen:

13. Make up a name for the animal based on its adaptations. _____

14. Now identify the animal using _A Field Guide to Pond Life._ _____

Amphibians alive!

Subjects
Science, art.

Concepts

Science skills
Observing, sequencing.

Focus
By making a temporary minipond habitat and watching the metamorphosis of a tadpole, get a close look at what an amphibian needs to stay alive. What are the different habitat requirements for the stages in a frog or toad's life cycle?

Did you know?
Amphibians have adapted to live on land but spend at least part of their lives in water or other moist places where they mate and lay eggs. Toads and frogs lay jelly-coated eggs in the water, which soon change into swimming, water-breathing tadpoles. After feeding on algae and other plant material in the water, they mature into air-breathing adult toads or frogs that eat insects.

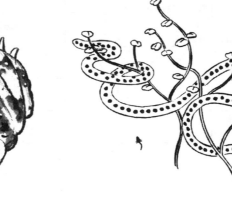

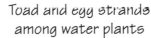

Toad and egg strands among water plants

What you need
❑ Small mesh net
❑ 1-gallon container with large opening (no soap residue)
❑ Plastic bag
❑ Piece of wood or bark
❑ Water scoop made from empty milk jug
❑ Amphibians Alive! Activity Sheet

Before you start
❑ Do this activity in the late spring or early summer.
❑ Always use a buddy system when exploring near water.

AMPHIBIANS ALIVE! ACTIVITY SHEET

Nature detective's name

Date

Observe the changes as the tadpole grows.
Draw the stages in an amphibian's life cycle.

Date:

Date:

Date:

Date:

Date:

Date:

Date:

Date:

Small
tadpole

Egg

Adult

Life
Cycle

No tail

Growing
tadpole

Grows
back legs

Grows
front legs

 ---------- Cut here and tape to Minipond ---------- ✂

TEMPORARY
MINIPOND HABITAT

*I promise to care for the inhabitants and
return them to a suitable ditch or pond's
edge when they are ready for life on land.*

Nature detective's signature

Date

What you do

1. At a wonderful wet place nearby, listen at night for loud croaking as frogs or toads call to their mates. The next day, look in the water for toad eggs in jelly strands or frog eggs in jelly clusters among the plants near the water's edge. If eggs are not found, there's still a good chance there are tadpoles swimming nearby.

2. Scoop up some water from the habitat. Collect a few eggs or tadpoles with the net. Don't let them dry out. Put them into the water in the scoop. Dig up some mud and a few small aquatic plants and put them in the plastic bag. Floating plants or ones that grow completely underwater are best. Take all the specimens home to make a temporary minipond.

3. In the container, recreate the habitat where the specimens were collected. Put mud on the bottom, with plants rooted in it. Gently pour in some of the collected water and let it settle. Then carefully pour in the rest of the water and specimens. Float the piece of wood in the water to act as "dry land."

4. Put the minipond habitat in a bright spot, but not in direct sunlight so the water won't get too hot. Cover it with clear plastic wrap and poke holes in the top. This will let air in but keep out curious indoor critters.

5. Observe the changes in the tadpoles as they grow, and record the findings on the Amphibians Alive activity sheet. What will happen if you put too many specimens in the minipond?

6. The feeding of tadpoles depends on the stage of their development. Young tadpoles feed on the algae and other plants in the water that was collected. Add bits of boiled lettuce or spinach. When they begin to grow legs, they need more protein in their diet. Feed with one small chunk of dried dog food or some flake fish food; too much will spoil the water.

7. Replace about one-fourth of the water in the minipond with newly collected water from a pond or ditch about every seven days.

8. When the tadpoles have grown legs and no longer have a tail, they will climb out of the water. They will have completed their metamorphosis and are ready to be released back to the wonderful wet place. There they can find small insects to eat. (If you handle the tiny adults, be sure you don't have insect repellent or sunscreen on because amphibians absorb these chemicals through their skin.)

Summary

Because amphibians require both land and water habitats to complete their life cycle, they face unique challenges in the city. In cities, land is criss-crossed by roads, which makes it dangerous for amphibians to travel to water habitats. Hazards like lawn mowers, cars, pesticides, predators, and people await amphibians on the move. In urban areas where ponds usually do not dry up in summer, frogs do well. Bullfrogs thrive in nutrient-rich, murky city ponds with gently sloping sides. Most frogs stay closer to water than toads. Because their skin is drier than a frog's, toads can live farther from water.

Often toads are found in backyards and gardens on summer evenings. During the day they usually burrow underground where its cool and damp. A toad's life cycle requires a shorter time to complete than a frog's, so toads are able to successfully breed in urban puddles and ditches, which might dry up in summer's heat. Unlike most frogs, toads leave their wonderful wet place when they are still small. This adaptation helps them begin life on land before the water supply dries up.

Following through

Research information about the decline in the worldwide population of amphibians, including salamanders, frogs, and toads. Find out what makes amphibians so susceptible to acid rain, pesticides, herbicides, and other toxins in the environment. What causes acid rain? What do humans need to do to preserve healthy water habitats for amphibians?

Creeping crayfish!

Subject
Science.

Concepts

Science skills
Observing, describing, cause and effect.

Focus
What physical characteristics and behaviors does the crayfish have that make it a successful critter in the wonderful wet places near you?

Did you know?
Crayfish are part of the cleanup crew in ponds and other aquatic habitats. They are scavengers and hunt by scent at night. Crayfish help to keep water habitats clean by eating dead plants and animals they find lying on the bottom. As freshwater cousins of ocean-dwelling lobsters, crayfish are a favorite food of people and other predators at pond-side, such as raccoons, turtles, herons, snakes, frogs, and fish. There are over 200 different kinds of crayfish in North America.

Mud mounds as evidence of crayfish activity

What you need
- ❏ Long-handled net
- ❏ Uncooked bacon tied on long string
- ❏ Water scoop made from recycled milk jug
- ❏ Unused aquarium or large glass jar
- ❏ Creeping Crayfish Activity Sheet
- ❏ Pencil

Before you start
- ❏ Review safety rules when exploring near water. Use a buddy system.
- ❏ Wear old clothes; this could get messy.
- ❏ Crayfish can pinch so keep track of your fingers!

What you do
1. To find out if crayfish are active in the area, look for mud chimneys near a wonderful wet place. The chimney is made of mud balls that the crayfish piles up at the entrance of its burrow as it digs down into the mud until it finds water. Usually the burrow is 2 to 3 feet deep. Since crayfish are active at night, they should be "at home" during the day.

CREEPING CRAYFISH ACTIVITY SHEET

_____   _____
        Nature detective's name   Date

How many antennae does your crayfish have? _____

The antennae help the crayfish to feel its way
around and to sense food chemicals in the
water so that it can find things to eat.

Give the crayfish a small piece of bacon.
What body parts does it use to
hold its food? _____

How many eyes does the crayfish have? _____

The eyes are at the end of movable stalks. How does
this help the crayfish? _____

_____

What body parts does the crayfish use to walk
slowly forward? _____

How many walking legs does it have? _____

When you startle the crayfish, does it move
forward or backwards? _____

What body part does it use to escape quickly? _____

Put a leaf in with the crayfish. What does the crayfish do? Why? _____

_____

_____

What body parts does the crayfish use to defend itself? _____

_____

How many pinchers does the crayfish have?_____
If it loses one in a fight, it can eventually regrow another.

Describe other special features of the crayfish that make it well adapted to its habitat: _____

_____

_____

_____

_____

Pincher
(or claw)

Antenna

Eye

Walking
leg

Abdomen
(or tail)

Tail fan

2. Lower the bacon bait on the string into the burrow. Pull up slowly when you feel a tug. If it doesn't take the bait, try dredging the bottom of a pond or ditch with the net in the evening when they are actively scavenging for food. Collect a crayfish specimen and place it in the water scoop to transport it.

3. Set up a temporary observation station in an unused aquarium or big glass jar. Keep the crayfish in water collected from the pond or ditch, since it breathes with feathery gills located at the base segments of the walking legs. Put in four dead leaves and see what happens.

4. Using the Creeping Crayfish Activity Sheet as a guide, record observations about the specimen to see what adaptations to habitat can be discovered.

5. Keep it only for one week and then release the crayfish in the area of its burrow.

Summary

To survive, animals must adapt to their surroundings. The crayfish's gills allow it to breathe underwater or in mud where the gills can stay moist. The antennae have receptors that can sense food chemicals even in muddy water. Pinchers hold the food and defend against predators. The hard exoskeleton offers some protection to the body of the crayfish. By burrowing in the mud or darting backward through the water with flicks of its fan-shaped tail, it will try to escape when it senses danger. The crayfish's eyes are on the ends of movable stalks, which gives it a wide range of vision to detect motion of predators. Four pairs of legs carry the crayfish along on land or on the bottom of ponds and ditches.

Following through

Construct a model crayfish claw that really moves! A crayfish can cast off its appendages and regenerate them as it gets bigger and changes its outer shell.

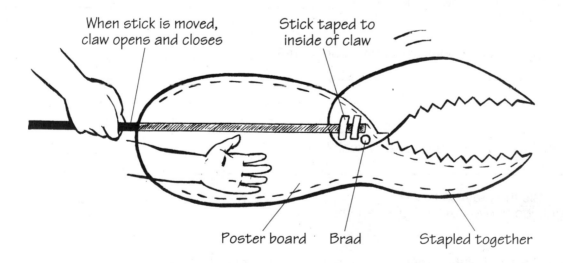

When stick is moved, claw opens and closes

Stick taped to inside of claw

Poster board   Brad   Stapled together

Telltale tracks

Subjects
Science, language arts.

Science skills
Observing, comparing and contrasting, discovering cause and effect.

Focus
The edge of a pond is a busy place. Resources (food, water, and shelter) from the land and water habitats are combined so many different plants and animals can be found there. What evidence of animal life can you discover by studying tracks on the banks of a wonderful wet place?

Did you know?
Many wild animals like the raccoon and opossum are active at night. Others, such as deer, are secretive to avoid predators. A fox is a shy but clever hunter. These behaviors make it hard for people to see animals so people do not always appreciate how many animals depend on certain habitats. Watching for clues like pathways and tracks helps determine what animals live in a community and how they use the habitat. Animals are creatures of habit; they often use the same routes again and again as they move between sources of food and water, burrows, temporary shelters, or good hiding places.

What you need

- ❑ Plaster of paris
- ❑ Water
- ❑ Cups (12-ounce size)
- ❑ Plastic spoons
- ❑ Cardboard strips (12" long by 3" wide)
- ❑ Stapler
- ❑ Newspaper
- ❑ Old toothbrushes
- ❑ Nature Detective Checklist (chapter 1)
- ❑ Telltale Tracks I.D. Sheet

Before you start

- ❑ Review safety rules for exploring near water.

What you do

1. Nature detectives explore the muddy area near a wonderful wet place to locate a track that is free of debris. Try to find out what animal made the footprint using the Telltale Tracks I.D. Sheet. Note the direction of the footprint and look for a trail.

2. To make a cast of the footprint, form a cardboard ring and fasten it with staples. Place the ring around the entire footprint and press it about 1" into the ground.

3. Spoon plaster into the mixing cup. Fill it to about 1½" from the top. Add water and stir with a spoon until the plaster mixture is about the thickness of pancake batter.

4. Gently pour the plaster mixture into the prepared cardboard ring. Fill the footprint first and then pour plaster until it is about 1" higher than the ground.

5. Let the cast harden for about one hour. When the plaster feels cool, pull up the cast by grasping the cardboard ring. Leave the ring on the cast for several hours while the plaster hardens completely. Wrap the dirty cast in newspaper to carry it.

6. Remove the ring and carefully break off any mud. Gently brush away dirt with a toothbrush.

7. Label the cast with the animal's identity, the collection site, and date.

8. Use the Nature Detective Checklist and make a journal of observations to go with the track casts.

Summary

Being able to "read" tracks can be like reading a nature story with the wild animals as the characters in the book. Identifying tracks tells which

TELLTALE TRACKS I.D. SHEET

_____   _____
Urban explorer's name   Habitat location

Which tracks can you find in a Wonderful Wet Place near you?
Measure the animal tracks you find and record the sizes.

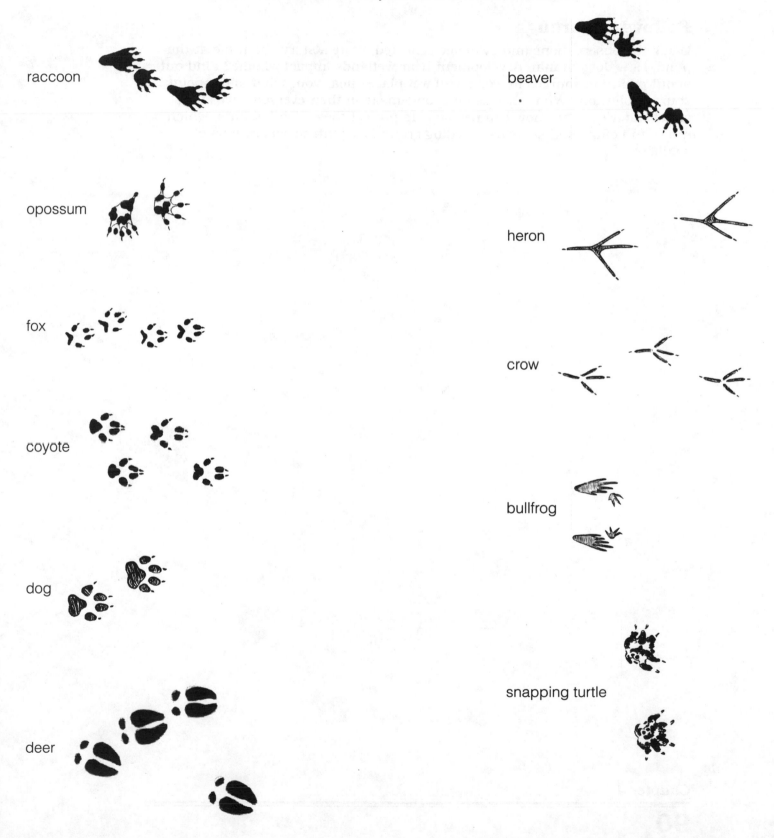

raccoon

opossum

fox

coyote

dog

deer

beaver

heron

crow

bullfrog

snapping turtle

characters are involved. Patterns of footprints and their direction can describe the action that takes place in the story. Was there a chase? Was the animal stalking prey or heading for a drink of water? Was it looking for the ripe berries on a bush? Tracks are important clues that can help solve the mystery about the roles of animals and plants within a community.

Following through

Using the observations and evidence collected, write a story about life at the pond. How does human development near wetlands impact wildlife? Find out about pollution sources in wonderful wet places near you. What is nonpoint source pollution? What choices do people make in their everyday lives that affect water quality? How can people help protect these rich habitats, which are so full of life and serve as breeding grounds for future generations of wildlife?

Suggested books

Downer, Ann. 1992. *Spring Pool*. New York: Franklin Watts.

> A beautiful explanation of temporary pools, which are important because they provide breeding and feeding grounds. Includes color photos of amphibian eggs.

Lyons, Janet and Jordan, Sandra. 1989. *Walking the Wetlands, Hiker's Guide to Common Plants/Animals of Marshes, Bogs & Swamps*. New York: John Wiley & Sons.

> Full-page line drawings and written descriptions of 100 plants and animals commonly found in freshwater habitats of the United States.

Nelson, Marie and Cindy Ellison. 1990. *WET Instruction Handbook*. Austin, Tex.: Texas Water Commission.

> This is the most comprehensive resource for understanding water quality that I have found. It provides specific guidelines for doing in-depth analysis of water habitats.

Parker, Steve. 1988. *Pond and River*. Eyewitness Series. New York: Alfred A. Knopf.

> This colorful pictorial reference to common pond plants and animals is an easy-to-read classroom reference book.

Slattery, Britt. 1991. *WOW-The Wonders of Wetlands*. St. Michaels, Md.: Environmental Concerns, Inc.

> Slattery has created a wonderful book packed full of information about every kind of wet place and numerous ways to explore them.

Thompson, Coldrey, & Bernard. 1984. *The Pond*. Oxford Scientific Books, Cambridge, Mass.: MIT Press.

> A book of amazing color photographs of pond animals and life cycles featuring a list of taxonomic orders and a color key to all the plants and animals featured.

Zim, Herbert. 1967. *Golden Guide to Pond Life*. New York: Golden Press.

> The classic, perfect book to carry as you go out to study wonderful, wet places. A must for all outdoor investigations.

Exploring backyards & schoolyards 5

City kids don't have to look in faraway places for nature. They just need to journey outside the back door to find a "jungle" of urban wildlife waiting to be discovered. If they lift a leaf, dig a hole, follow a butterfly, or feed a bird, they will connect with nature. Many people take for granted the critters in their own backyard. Even though worms, caterpillars, and pill bugs might not be thought of as wildlife because they are small, there are millions of them busy doing big jobs in nature. They are at work in everyone's neighborhood—in backyards and schoolyards.

Many wild animals that have been able to adapt to life in the city are active at night when most people sleep. Living under the cover of darkness, they have little contact with people. As a result, most urban homeowners and apartment dwellers do not realize they have such wild neighbors.

Animals such as raccoons, opossums, skunks, snakes, and spiders might be considered a nuisance as they make themselves at home in an attic or under a porch. But many people welcome wildlife—especially birds and butterflies—to their yards by planting native plants for food and shelter or using special feeders. Watching wildlife in a backyard habitat is a lot of fun. If kids take the time to observe closely, they might be amazed with their own homegrown wilderness. When they see ecological relationships in their own backyard, they will have more respect and appreciation for wildlife worldwide.

Habitat hunt

Subjects
Science, math.

Science skills
Observing, recording, comparing, and contrasting.

Focus
Animals often use what people have created. What critters will you find when you explore backyard or schoolyard habitats?

Did you know?

In city neighborhoods, insulated utility wires have become roads for rodents such as rats and squirrels. Balancing on the high wires is safer than crossing busy streets and allows them to feed within a larger area. Many birds such as sparrows, purple martins, doves, and  flycatchers also find that utility wires make a perfect perch for resting out of reach of most predators. The flycatchers and martins swoop down from the wires to capture flying insects. Hawks hunt small prey from atop tall utility poles. Animals that can survive near people sometimes use human-made structures instead of natural ones.

What you need
❑ Pencil and paper
❑ Habitat Hunt Activity Sheet
❑ Binoculars (optional)

What you do

1. Using the Habitat Hunt Activity Sheet, have urban explorers observe the wildlife in their own backyards before and after school for a three-day period. Circle or check the critters observed and record how many of each species was seen. On the back of the checklist, list any other animals not pictured.

2. On the same days, make observations on the school grounds in the early morning and midafternoon. Make a list of the critters seen and how many of each species.

3. Compare the observation results between the two habitats. Did the backyard or the schoolyard have the most animals? Which one offers the most opportunities for wildlife? Which habitat has the most diversity? What was the best time to see animals? Ask the urban explorers to explain how their backyards differ from the schoolyard habitat.

Chapter 5

HABITAT HUNT ACTIVITY SHEET

Urban explorer's name

Date

What critters can you find in your own backyard?

Draw or note any other living things you discover and where you saw them.

Spider
Eats: flying insects such as flies and moths

Bumblebee
Eats: nectar and pollen

Gecko lizard Eats: insects

Hummingbird
Eats: flower nectar

Butterfly
Eats: flower nectar

Cedar waxwing
Eats: berries, seeds

Praying mantis
Eats: insects

Blue jay
Eats: seeds and insects

Earthworm
Eats: dead plants and soil

Slug
Eats: living or dead plants

Centipede
Eats: slugs, insects, worms

Squirrel
Eats: nuts, seeds, and fungi

Chimney swift
Eats: flying insects

Pond

Opossum
Eats: people's leftovers

Toad
Eats: flying insects, worms

Bat
Eats: mosquitoes, moths

Raccoon
Eats: people's leftovers, bird eggs, berries

Mourning dove
Eats: seeds

Mockingbird
Eats: insects, berries

4. To find nighttime critters, settle into a spot 15 minutes before sunset and be very still and quiet. Wait, watch, and listen as the nighttime animals become active when the sun begins to set.

5. Have each child draw a "bird's eye view" map of his or her own backyard, noting where critters were located. Then the child can compare his or her map with other urban explorers and discuss the similarities and differences in the backyard habitats.

6. What threats do animals face in backyards and schoolyard habitats? What benefits do animals have when using structures made by people? What changes can be made in the habitats to encourage a variety of critters to come to your school or backyard?

Summary

Even though there are some similarities between schoolyards and backyards, more people and less diversity of landscaping in schoolyards make a difference to some species of animals. The lack of a consistent source of water on school grounds is an important limiting factor for wildlife. Children might be surprised to find out that nighttime critters such as bats, nighthawks, moths, rats, owls, raccoons, and opossums share their neighborhood.

Following through

Do the activities in chapter 6, "Nurturing nature close to home," to enhance schoolyard and backyard habitats for wildlife. Repeat the habitat hunt after six months to see how many more species of animals have been attracted to the "new, improved" site.

Food factory

Subjects
Science, art.

Science skills
Observing, recording, comparing, and contrasting.

Focus
A diversity of plant life supports a diverse and healthy wildlife population. How many different kinds of leaves will you find in your backyard or schoolyard?

Did you know?
Green leaves are food factories for plants. The leaves take in CO_2 and water and absorb light energy from the sun to produce the sugars needed for plant growth. This process is called *photosynthesis* (meaning "to make from light"). When animals eat plants, they get energy from the sugars in the plant. Food energy is then transferred to the animals that consume the plant-eaters. Plants are the "green machines" that power the food energy systems on earth.

Food chain

What you need
❑ Food Factory Activity Sheet
❑ Pencil
❑ Unprinted newspaper sheets
❑ Crayons (with paper removed)

Before you start
❑ Know how to identify and avoid poison ivy, poison oak, and poison sumac.

Poison oak

Poison ivy

Poison sumac

FOOD FACTORY ACTIVITY SHEET

_____   _____
Urban explorer's name   Date

Leaves are food factories for green plants. Some animals get their energy from eating plants.
Look for these leaf shapes and record the types found.
Which ones show evidence of being food for animals?

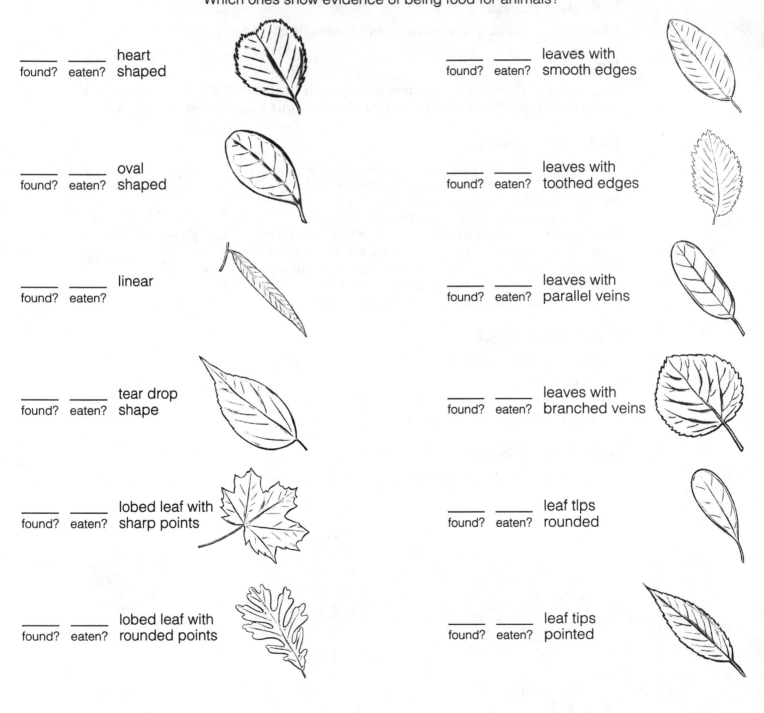

_____ _____ heart
found? eaten? shaped

_____ _____ oval
found? eaten? shaped

_____ _____ linear
found? eaten?

_____ _____ tear drop
found? eaten? shape

_____ _____ lobed leaf with
found? eaten? sharp points

_____ _____ lobed leaf with
found? eaten? rounded points

_____ _____ other
found? eaten? (Draw in leaf.)

_____ _____ leaves with
found? eaten? smooth edges

_____ _____ leaves with
found? eaten? toothed edges

_____ _____ leaves with
found? eaten? parallel veins

_____ _____ leaves with
found? eaten? branched veins

_____ _____ leaf tips
found? eaten? rounded

_____ _____ leaf tips
found? eaten? pointed

_____ _____ other
found? eaten? (Draw in leaf.)

What you do

1. Search the backyard or school grounds to discover the diversity of plant life.

2. Examine leaves using the Food Factory Activity Sheet to look for the various leaf characteristics.

3. Make a check mark by each one found. In the spaces provided or on the back of the activity sheet, draw any leaf that is not already pictured.

4. Indicate which leaves show evidence of being a food source to an animal. How can you tell?

5. What other parts of the plants can animals use as food? Did you find berries, nuts, flowers with nectar, pollen, sap?

Summary

Looking closely at leaf shapes is a way to appreciate the diversity of plant life. Plants that show evidence of being eaten are more likely to be plants that are native to the area. The plants that have evolved and occur naturally in your area are best suited to provide food for local wildlife.

Following through

Collect a variety of shapes of leaves. Have children share leaves or use fallen leaves to reduce the number taken from nature. Arrange the leaves under blank newspaper and rub with the side of crayons. The design created can be used as gift wrapping and stationery. Put the leaves back outside or on a compost pile. A collection of leaf-rubbing pages can be kept like a journal. Use the leaf journal and a field guide to learn more about plants in your area.

Leaf litter critters

Subject

Science.

Science skills

Observing, cause and effect, recording.

Focus

Pill bugs have adapted to life in leaf litter habitats. What is the pill bug's role in nature?

Concepts

Did you know?

The small, grey pill bug is not a bug at all. It is a crustacean that is related to lobsters, crabs, and shrimp. Like its aquatic relatives, the pill bug breathes with gills but has adapted to live on land. Its two long antennae help to seek out suitable habitats by acting as humidity detectors. There are two taillike tubes at the end of its body that can pick up water and send it to the gills. These critters have many names. Scientists refer to them as isopods, but people who know them as familiar backyard creatures often call them roly-polys, doodle bugs, wood lice, sow bugs, and of course, pill bugs.

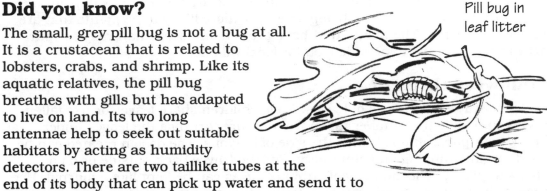

Pill bug in leaf litter

What you need

- ❑ 2 shoe boxes with lids
- ❑ Spoon
- ❑ Damp paper towel
- ❑ Spray bottle with water
- ❑ Black construction paper
- ❑ Hand lens
- ❑ Timer or watch
- ❑ Dead leaf
- ❑ Styrofoam cup
- ❑ Leaf Litter Critter Activity Sheet

Before you start

- ❑ When looking under things for specimens, be cautious of critters that sting or bite to defend themselves.

LEAF LITTER CRITTER ACTIVITY SHEET

_____   _____
Urban explorer's name   Date

Cut and staple these pages to make a minijournal.
Record the findings based on the experimental activities with the pill bugs.

LEAF LITTER
MINIJOURNAL

by _____
                Name

Pill Bug's Address:

_____

_____

Draw a picture of the pill bug.

Count how many legs.

Draw a picture of the pill bug's
reaction to touch.

Pill Bug Preference:

_____ moist   _____ dry

Pill Bug Preference:

_____ light   _____ dark

Draw the leaf.

Day 1

Day 3

Daily Decomposer Diet
Record items eaten:

_____ paper   _____ styrofoam   _____ ketchup
                        cups   packets

_____ fallen   _____ dead   _____ straws
        leaves   plants

_____ other

The End

Draw a pill bug portrait.

What you do

1. Collect six pill bugs in a plastic cup from under rocks, bricks, boards, or leaf litter on the ground. Put a little dirt and a dead leaf in the cup.

2. Using a hand lens, observe the pill bugs in the plastic cup. Do the following experiments and record the findings in the pages of the Leaf Litter Critter minijournal.

3. Why do you think this critter is nicknamed "roly-poly?" What does the pill bug do when it is touched gently? How do you think this reaction helps the pill bug?

4. Put a damp paper towel covering half of the bottom of a shoe box. With a spoon, place the six pill bugs into the dry side of the box. Cover the entire box with the lid. Wait 5 minutes and then look in the box. Where are the pill bugs?

5. Now remove the paper towel. Mist the whole box. Note the location of the pill bugs. Using black paper, make half of the box light and half dark by covering one end. Check the box at 10-minute intervals to see where the pill bugs are. How does the light difference affect their location?

6. Cover the bottom of the box with the damp paper towel again. Place the dead leaf (without holes) in the box. Observe for a few minutes to see how the pill bugs react to the leaf. Put the lid on the box and poke a few holes in it for air. Keep the temporary habitat moist by misting the paper towel as needed. For the next two days, check the leaf and the pill bugs. Are they eating the leaf? Is there anything else in the box now?

7. Create the same habitat in another shoe box. Lift out three of the pill bugs with a spoon and place them in the new box. Instead of a leaf, put in a styrofoam cup, some bits of notebook paper, and two or three other pieces of litter found on the ground outside. For two days, watch for signs of eating. Do the pill bugs eat the trash if leaf litter is not available?

8. Return the pill bugs back to nature when observations are finished.

Summary

The experiments show how these crustaceans have adapted to life on land. They seek dark, moist places—a response that keeps them from drying out during the day as they seek cover under leaves at the surface of the soil. Rolling up in a ball protects the pill bug from attack by predators such as spiders and ants. The gills are also protected from drying out when the critter rolls up in a tight little ball. (Note: Sow bugs look similar but are a different species of isopod, and they cannot roll up.) If there are droppings in the box, that is evidence that pill bugs eat leaves. Their role in nature is as a decomposer of dead plants, returning nutrients to the soil in their droppings. Some pill bugs have been observed eating trash such as paper and even styrofoam cups.

Following through

Set up a habitat in an old aquarium for a longer look at the life cycle of the pill bug. Feed them bits of vegetable matter from lunch leftovers. Watch for interesting behaviors such as how they carry their eggs underneath their bodies and shed their skins as they grow.

Worm world

Subject
Science.

Concepts

Science skills
Observation, discovering cause and effect.

Focus
By setting up a temporary habitat, it is possible to explore the hidden world of the worm. What evidence does the worm world reveal about the beneficial effects of earthworms in the soil?

Did you know?
An earthworm does not have eyes. Instead, it has light-sensitive cells in its skin. Having more light-sensing cells in the front end of its body helps it find the soil surface. But sunshine can kill the nerve endings in the worm's skin, so exposure at the surface can leave it paralyzed. Sometimes large numbers of earthworms evacuate the safety of their dark, underground habitat after a heavy rainfall. They soak up air through their slimy skin, which must stay moist, but when their tunnels are flooded, they have a hard time breathing. They crawl to the surface to get air, but they often die from exposure or get eaten.

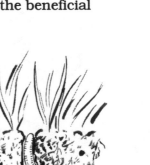

Earthworm

What you need
- ❑ Shoe box
- ❑ Empty 3-liter soda bottle with top cut off
- ❑ Black plastic trash bag and rubber band
- ❑ Tape
- ❑ Garden soil
- ❑ Sand
- ❑ Dead leaves and grass clippings
- ❑ Water
- ❑ Hand lens
- ❑ Flashlight
- ❑ Timer or watch

Before you start
- ❑ Collect three earthworms using the following methods:
  - • At night, using a flashlight covered with red cellophane, sneak up on earthworms feeding at the soil surface. They can feel the vibrations caused by footsteps, so walk softly.

- During the day, dig for worms in moist soil where there are small crusty lumps ("castings") piled at the surface. If the soil is very dry, worms might be 3 feet under!

❑ Put the worms in a shoe box with a damp paper towel and some dirt, and keep the lid on.

What you do

1. To make the worm world, put alternating 1" layers of soil and sand in the jar. Sprinkle drops of water on each layer as you fill the jar about ¾ full. Add dead leaves and grass clippings.

2. Tape black plastic around the entire jar. Make a journal for recording observations.

3. Before you place the worms in their temporary home, observe them in the shoe box. Record the observations in a journal. Can you tell the difference between the head and the rear end? (The head end usually goes first when the worm crawls.) How does the worm's shape change as it moves? Gently stroke the worm up one side and down the other. Does it feel the same in both directions? With a hand lens, look at the tiny bristles on each segment of the worm. What do you think the bristles help the worm do?

4. Put one of the worms in the jar. How long does it take the worm to burrow out of sight? Now put another worm in the jar and shine the flashlight on the worm. How does it react? How does its burrowing time differ from the first worm?

5. When all the worm specimens are in the jar, cover it with a circle cut from the black plastic trash bag. Secure the top with a rubber band and poke some holes in the plastic for air. Keep the worm world in a cool place.

6. Remove the black paper every day to make observations of the worm world. What has happened to the dried leaves and grass clippings? How many tunnels can you see? Describe the movements of the worms.

7. As needed, feed the worms dead leaves, grass clippings, and small bits of vegetable scraps from lunch leftovers. Which foods do the worms seem to like best? Sprinkle a few drops of water on the soil daily.

8. What has happened to the soil and sand layers? How long did it take for the worms to mix the layers? Are worm droppings (castings) deposited at the soil surface?

9. Keep the "worm world" no longer than two weeks. In nature, if the soil becomes too dry or too wet, the worms will move to a new place. They can't do that in the jar, so release them in your backyard or a suitable schoolyard habitat.

Summary

Earthworms work the soil and recycle nutrients to the earth. The layers of soil and sand were mixed by the worms' movements. In the worm world, the black paper kept out light and encouraged worm activity near the jar sides. The worms' activity showed how they eat their way through the soil, leaving tunnels, which allow air into the soil. This helps plants grow better since plant roots need oxygen. When rainwater trickles down the tunnels, plant roots can soak up nutrients in the soil that are dissolved in the water. As earthworms eat decaying matter, they digest what they need to live and deposit their droppings at the surface. These castings contain important nutrients that enrich the soil and make it a good habitat for plants and other soil critters.

Following through

Save space in local landfills by setting up a worm bin at school or in your own backyard. Let the worms do the work of composting vegetable waste from school lunches or your family's kitchen. Use the compost as a natural fertilizer in a garden. Look in the resource list at the back of this book to find out where to order red worms and worm bins. Build your own worm bin with plans obtained from a local nature center or agricultural extension office.

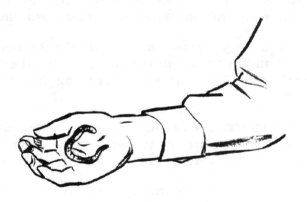

Caterpillar caper

Subject
Science.

Science skills
Observing, cause and effect, sequencing, recording.

Focus
A homemade hatching habitat provides a window to watch the metamorphosis of a caterpillar to a butterfly. What habitat requirements do butterflies have to be able to complete their life cycle?

Did you know?
While most adult butterflies might visit many different types of flowers in search of nectar, their larvae (caterpillars) are very picky eaters. Specific plants act as "host" plants for the hungry larvae, and female butterflies will only lay their eggs on those plants. A female often uses sense organs on her feet to tell whether or not to deposit her eggs on a plant. By scratching and tapping the leaf in a drumming motion, the female butterfly tastes the leaf with her feet to find out if it is a suitable host plant that can be eaten by the caterpillars when they hatch from the eggs.

Monarch laying eggs on milkweed

What you need
- ❑ Cardboard box (about 18" × 12")
- ❑ Clear plastic wrap
- ❑ Tape
- ❑ Scissors and pencil
- ❑ Jar of water
- ❑ Caterpillar Caper Activity Sheet
- ❑ Butterfly eggs or caterpillar

Before you start
- ❑ In spring, follow a butterfly that is fluttering and then touching down on green plants.
- ❑ Watch to see if it is a female laying her eggs on the leaves.
- ❑ Collect the tiny eggs by picking a sprig of the host plant.
- ❑ If a caterpillar is collected and you are not sure it was on the host plant, pick a variety of leaves from the area and observe which type it eats.

What you do

1. To make the hatching habitat box, cut the bottom and top out of the cardboard box or push in the flaps so there are two large open sides. Cut a flap in the side of the box that is large enough for a hand and supplies to go through. Poke a few small air holes in the top of the box.

2. Cover the bottom of the hatching habitat with a damp paper towel. A humid environment makes it easier for the caterpillars to breathe through the tiny holes in the sides of their bodies called *spiracles*.

3. Fill a short jar with water and cover it with plastic wrap. Place it in the hatching habitat. Poke the stem of the host plant through the plastic into the water. This keeps the plant from wilting and the caterpillars from crawling into the water and drowning.

4. Now place any individually collected leaves on the bottom of the box. Prop a few sticks against the cardboard sides for the caterpillar to crawl on when it is ready to pupate.

5. After putting in the collected egg or caterpillar specimens, cover both open sides of the hatching habitat with clear plastic wrap taped to the box.

Clear plastic on both sides of box

Hatching habitat box

6. Temperature is important to developing insect larvae. Keep the box out of direct sunlight but in a warm place that is about the same as the average outdoor temperature.

7. Use the Caterpillar Caper Activity Sheet as you make observations about the behavior and physical characteristics of the different life stages of the butterfly. Add leaves for food as needed and put a clean, damp paper towel in the bottom of the hatching habitat daily.

8. Soon after the butterfly has hatched from its chrysalis and its wings have dried, take the hatching habitat to a flower garden and release the new butterfly back to nature.

CATERPILLAR CAPER ACTIVITY SHEET

_____   _____
Urban explorer's name   Date

Draw in the stages of the butterfly's life cycle as you observe them in the hatching habitat.
The metamorphosis ("change of form") may take as long as six weeks.

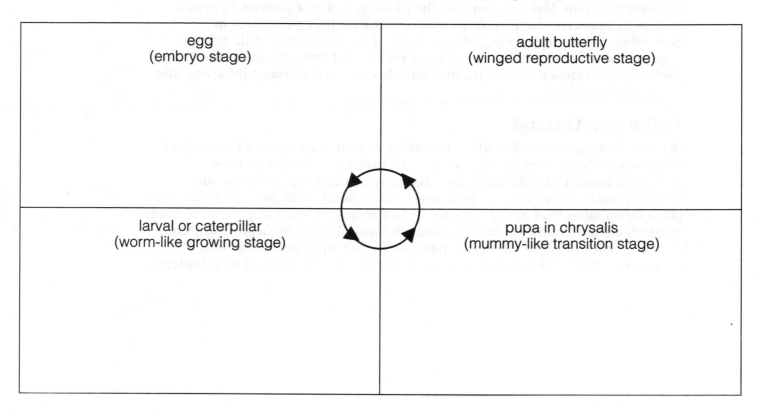

| egg (embryo stage) | adult butterfly (winged reproductive stage) |
| larval or caterpillar (worm-like growing stage) | pupa in chrysalis (mummy-like transition stage) |

RECORD BEHAVIORS AND PHYSICAL CHANGES BELOW:

1. When did the egg hatch? _____

2. What is the length of the newly hatched caterpillar? _____

3. How many times did the caterpillar shed its skin as it grew? _____

4. What is the length of the caterpillar just before it pupated? _____

5. When did it transform into a pupa? _____

6. The pupa stage lasted _____ days.

7. When did the adult butterfly emerge from its chrysalis? _____

8. The butterfly was released back to a suitable natural habitat on _____

OTHER THINGS I NOTICED: _____

_____

_____

_____

_____

_____

Summary

Observing the life cycle of a caterpillar as it transforms into a butterfly is a beautiful illustration of relationships between specific plants and the species of butterflies that depend on them. These relationships have evolved through a multitude of generations. Butterflies are suffering from a loss of habitat because of urban development and the plowing under of prairies to create cropland. Pesticide use is another cause of the declining numbers of butterflies. By understanding the life cycle of the butterfly and its habitat requirements, we can help by providing nectar and larval foods in our backyards to replace the plants that have been removed from wild areas that are being developed.

Following through

Set up a feeding station for adult butterflies in your yard by planting some of these sun-loving nectar plants: black-eyed Susan, gay-feather, pentas, coreopsis, aster, butterfly weed, lantana, purple coneflower, verbena, and butterfly bush. To help future generations of butterflies complete their life cycle, plant larval foods that are specific to the butterflies common in your area. Some suggestions are: milkweed for the monarch butterfly; dill, fennel and Queen Anne's lace for black swallowtails; pipevine for the pipevine swallowtail; passionvine for the gulf fritillary butterfly; thistles for the painted lady butterfly.

Bee business

Subject
Science.

Science skills
Observing, classifying.

Focus
Bees are beneficial insects that can be found "working" in your backyard or schoolyard. What job do they do in nature?

Did you know?
Bees of all kinds are important pollinators of flowering plants. When pollen is exchanged between plants of the same species, the plants can form seeds, which are the packages of life for the plant's next generation. While bees are looking for nectar, the powdery, yellow pollen in the flowers sticks to the tiny hairs on their body. With bristlelike hairs on their back legs, the bees comb their bodies and pack the collected pollen into "pollen baskets" on each back leg. Pollen is a high-protein food for bees.

Concepts

Bumblebee with full pollen baskets

What you need
- ❏ Bee Business Activity Sheet
- ❏ Pencil
- ❏ Floral tape
- ❏ Black pipe cleaners
- ❏ Thin wire
- ❏ Microscope (optional)

Before you start
- ❏ If a bee comes too close for comfort, stand still or move slowly away. Bees might sting to defend themselves when threatened by swatting hands. Otherwise, they are not out to get people.
- ❏ This is a spring or summer activity.

What you do
1. Make a "bee tongue" with a 1-inch piece of wire wrapped in sticky floral tape. Then make a "bee-sized body" from a black pipe cleaner with a piece left sticking out as a handle. Attach the sticky wire piece to the pipe cleaner bee.

2. Have the kids go outside with their "bees" and find flowers. As the children pretend they are honeybees gathering nectar from flowers, check to see

BEE BUSINESS ACTIVITY SHEET

_____   _____
Urban explorer's name   Date

There are different types of bees with different shapes, sizes and behaviors. All bees are insects with 3 body parts, 6 legs, and 2 pair of wings. What bees are busy working in your backyard or schoolyard?

CHECK OFF THE TYPES OF BEES YOU OBSERVE:

Honeybee

Carpenter bee

Bumblebee

Leaf-cutting bee

Sweat bee

Honey bees are social insects, with a variety of jobs divided among the 60,000 members of a hive. All the honey bees seen gathering nectar and pollen are female worker bees that are between 26–42 days old. Worker bees only live 6 weeks. Not all types of bees are social insects.

Flowers have adapted ways of attracting bees with flower nectar, coloration and shape.

DRAW SOME SHAPES OF FLOWERS THAT OFFER GOOD LANDING AND CRAWLING SPACES:

RECORD THE NUMBERS OF BEES SEEN ON:

white flowers _____   blue flowers _____   red flowers _____   yellow flowers _____

orange flowers _____   purple flowers _____

WATCH FOR OTHER BEE BEHAVIORS:

How many bees are seen: hovering? _____   walking or sitting on flowers? _____

Drinking nectar? _____   With full pollen baskets? _____

With pollen on their body hairs? _____   Attacking enemies? _____

what else has been collected on their "tongues" and "bodies." Did the "bee" visit several flowers of the same species? If so, it was acting as a pollinator.

3. If possible, have a closer look under a microscope at what the children find attached to their "bees."

4. Using the Bee Business Activity Sheet, record observations about real bees and their activity in a backyard or schoolyard.

Summary

Bee business is big business to people. Without bees as pollinators of many important crops, people would not be able to grow the large quantities of fruits, vegetables, and nuts that we find in our grocery stores. Many plants depend on bees to be able to make their seeds. Those seeds make more plants that in turn feed animals that eat plant products such as berries, fruits, seeds, and nuts. Flowers have adapted to attract pollinators. Bees are found most often on blue, white, and yellow flowers. They cannot see the color red. Some flowers have coloration on their petals called nectar guides that appear as an attractive "landing strip" to airborne bees. Bees prefer flower shapes that offer crawling and sitting space as they gather nectar and pollen. Bees do important work in nature as part of the interdependent community.

Following through

Celebrate the useful things that bees make. Honeybees make wax inside their bodies. They excrete bits of wax and then shape it into six-sided storage cells in the hive. People use the wax as an ingredient in food and art supplies, makeup, lipstick, and lotions. It might take a hive of honeybees 50,000 trips to collect enough flower nectar to make a pound of honey! Have a tasting party of local honey varieties. Light up some bee's wax candles to make it festive!

Backyard bird banquet

Subject
Science.

Science skills
Observing, recording, comparing, and contrasting.

Focus
Birds have adaptations that allow them to eat certain foods. How many different species of birds will your backyard banquet attract?

Did you know?

Bluejay

The Audubon Society says that people in the United States spend $90 million a year feeding birds in their backyards. Some people record their observations at the backyard feeder and report their sightings to scientists in conservation organizations. Bird watchers enjoy getting to know the behaviors of different species. It's fun to see blue jays stuff their cheeks with food and then fly to a perch to eat. With tiny feet, chickadees and titmice hold seeds against a branch as they peck away the outer shells. Goldfinches often crowd feeders in hungry flocks of 20 to 30 birds at a time. Other birds might fly away from a feeder when a cardinal announces its approach with a strong, loud cheep. Backyard birds are entertaining.

Before you start
❑ Put up any pets during the feeding activity.
❑ Remove any other feeders in the yard for the day. If birds have not been fed in the yard before, it might take a few days to attract them.
❑ This activity can also be done in a schoolyard.

What you need
❑ 6 foods: corn, sunflower seeds, bread, whole peanuts, millet, berries/fruit (collected or purchased)
❑ 6 shoe-box lids
❑ Binoculars (optional)
❑ Backyard Bird Banquet Activity Sheet and pencil
❑ *A Field Guide to Birds*

What you do
1. Set up the bird banquet on the ground in an open area where the bird activity can be easily watched. Put equal amounts of each type of food in each shoe-box lid. Weight the feeding tray down so it won't blow away. Listen for bird sounds as they call other birds to "come and get it." Observe

BACKYARD BIRD BANQUET ACTIVITY SHEET

Name _____

Habitat _____

Identify banquet guests.
Check off foods selected
by each species.

Date _____

Weather _____

BANQUET MENU

GUEST LIST	corn	sunflower seeds	peanuts	bread	millet seeds	berries/fruit
TOTALS:						

OTHER BIRDS OBSERVED IN THE YARD: What do you think they eat?

_____

_____

_____

HOW DO FOOD CHOICES RELATE TO BIRD BEAK SHAPE?
(Draw and color in as a bar graph.)

# of birds
with these
beaks
seen at
feeder

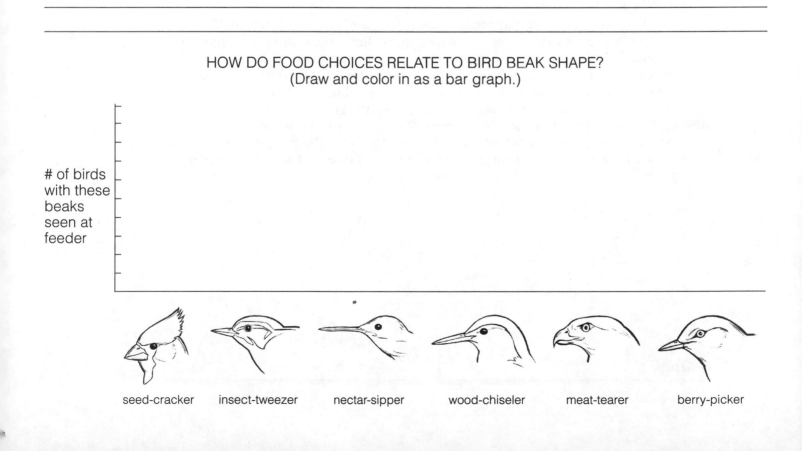

seed-cracker   insect-tweezer   nectar-sipper   wood-chiseler   meat-tearer   berry-picker

Listen for bird sounds as they call other birds to "come and get it." Observe the activity at the feeding trays throughout the day.

2. Identify the birds with a field guide. Using the Bird Banquet Activity Sheet, record the birds and the foods they selected. What was the most popular food?

3. Fill in the bird beak chart on the activity sheet to record how the birds' food choices relate to their beak shape. Flip through the *Field Guide to Birds* and look at the beaks of birds. What types of birds would you not expect to find attending the bird banquet?

4. What time of day were birds most active? Were any new species of birds attracted by the bird banquet? What other kinds of animals were seen at the feeding trays?

5. Were other birds observed in the yard that did not come to the banquet? What was on their menu?

6. The next day, fill a seed feeder with millet and sunflower seeds and hang it near the feeding trays. Fill only one feeding tray with the same seed mixture as the hanging feeder. Remove the other trays. Which birds prefer the hanging feeder? Which prefer feeding on the ground?

Summary

Birds are busiest in the early morning and early evening, as they search for fuel for their active bodies, which burn up energy quickly. Their beaks are adapted as tools that they use to get their food. Some beaks are nutcrackers, insect-tweezers, seed-crunchers, berry-pickers, and nectar-sippers. To encourage diversity of species, a backyard or schoolyard feeding program needs to provide food, water, shelter, and cover with natural plantings and specialized food containers. To attract certain species, food preferences and bird behavior determine the placement and types of food to use.

Following through

Try the bird banquet during another season and see how the "guest list" varies. Look for ways to increase your bird guest list. Some birds are not only picky about what they eat, but also how and where they feed. Contact a local nature center or library to get easy designs for feeders made from recycled materials. To attract insect-eating birds such as warblers, robins, mockingbirds, and wrens, use yard pesticides sparingly or not at all. Woodpeckers appreciate dead trees where they can find wood-boring insects. If old limbs on trees aren't a safety hazard, leave them for the birds to explore for bugs. Look for a work crew that is removing a dead tree and take it home to "plant" in the ground as an instant woodpecker habitat.

Suggested books

Burnett, Robin. 1992. *The Pillbug Project, A guide to investigation*. Washington, D.C.: National Science Teachers Foundation.

> A very interesting and complete curriculum for studying pill bugs.

Echols, Jean. 1987. *Buzzing a Hive*. Berkeley, Calif.: Lawrence Hall of Science, University of California.

> A teacher's guide with six lesson plans about bees and wonderful reproducibles.

Hand, Julia. 1995 *The Wonderful World of Wigglers*. Vt.: Common Roots Press.

> Activities with worms that involve kids in solving real-life problems using critical and creative thinking.

Hickman, Pamela. 1992. *Bird Wise*. Reading, Mass.: Addison-Wesley Publishing Company.

> A well-planned book with good information about birds and wonderful activities to help your kids learn how to observe them.

Hickman, Pamela. 1991. *Plant Wise*. Toronto: Kids Can Press.

> Hickman provides excellent activities for kids for an extended study about plants.

Kneidel, Sally. 1994. *Pet Bugs*. New York: John Wiley & Sons, Inc.

> This book is an excellent resource for planning range observation of small wildlife.

Kneidel, Sally. 1993. *Creepy Crawlies and the Scientific Method*. Golden, Colo.: Fulcrum Press.

> Kneidel describes well-thought-out science experiments with small urban wildlife.

Kramer, David C. 1989. *Animals in the Classroom*. Menlo Park, Calif.: Addison-Wesley Publishing Company.

> If you decide to keep small animals in your classroom, this book will show you how to do it right.

McLaughlin, Molly. 1986. *Earthworms, Dirt and Rotten Leaves*. New York: Atheneum.

> This book has easy-to-read, detailed information and graphics about earthworms.

Mitchell, John. 1985. *Field Guide to Your Own Backyard*. New York: W.W. Norton & Co.

> This interesting book will send you out into your own backyard with a new sense of understanding and curiosity.

Nurturing nature close to home

6

After investigating different habitats in their city, kids will have a better appreciation for the need to save a place for nature close to home. City critters and migrating animals can be helped by people who view their yards as habitats. As more people choose native garden plants that have value to wildlife, little by little, people are reconnecting patches of land—backyard to backyard—and improving habitat opportunities for a wider variety of animals.

As families choose how they care for their yards, how they clean their houses, and what types of products they buy, they can have more combined impact on the environment than big industry. Conservation needs to begin at home, where kids can learn to do their small part for the earth. When kids share the responsibility for clean, healthy habitats and feel that they are part of the solution to the threatened loss of natural resources, then they will have more hope for the future.

These committed urban explorers can recruit other kids to form a conservation crew and get involved in environmental projects in their hometown to save species and habitats before they become endangered. By encouraging action that benefits wildlife, there can be more balance between human needs and animal needs. That approach will create a better habitat for all living things—wild animals, plants, and people.

Habitat helpers

Subject
Science.

Concepts

Science skills
Observing, recording, and predicting.

Focus
Take a look at your yard from a wild animal's point of view. What can you do to help create or restore habitat for more critters?

Did you know?
Habitat loss is the main reason that plants and animals become extinct or endangered. Because of land development in central Texas, the golden-cheeked warbler is running out of room. The warbler is picky; it only uses bark from old ashe juniper trees for its nesting material and only eats bugs found in oak trees. But many oak trees in the breeding area are dying out and not being replaced. People cut and burn ashe juniper trees to clear their land. Since the endangered golden-cheeked warbler is a "habitat specialist," it can't just move somewhere else to live.

Golden-cheeked warbler

People in conservation groups are helping preserve habitats for the warbler and other endangered species. Some animals need big help to save large tracts of wild land. Others can be helped in habitats as small as your backyard.

What you need
❑ Habitat Helpers Checklist
❑ Pencil and paper
❑ Red pencil or pen

What you do
1. To become a habitat helper, first look at your yard from a wild animal's point of view. If you were a woodpecker, a lizard, or a raccoon, where would you find food, water, shelter, and a place to raise a family? Using the pencil and paper, make a "bird's eye view" map of your yard, showing the things that attract wildlife. Show your house, garage, and other structures. Which spaces are used by animals? Do any of the structures seem to keep wildlife from coming to the area? Don't forget fences, gates, sidewalks, and driveways.

2. On the back of the map, make a list of all the animals you can remember that have come to your yard.

3. On the Habitat Helpers Checklist, decide what new critters that you want to attract. Some species will be drawn in by the right food and water sources; others might also want a place to raise a family.

4. Think about how your family's backyard activities blend with the needs and activities of the animals you want to invite over. Are there any hazards to wildlife in your yard? Does your family use insecticides?

5. Read about the lifestyles of the animals you want to come to your habitat. Find out their likes and dislikes.

6. Using the Habitat Helpers Checklist, do a "walk-through" of the yard. Put a check mark by the things you want to add to attract those animals. Here are some ideas to think about: Do you want to put in a sunny garden with flowers for butterflies? Do you want to grow vines on a fence to offer tubular-shaped flowers to hummingbirds? Do you have an open space where a purple martin house can be put up? Can you attract migratory songbirds with water sources? If you have too many mosquitoes, would you like to mount a bat house up in a tree?

7. Get your map and use a red pencil to draw in the things you want to change or add so you can get busy as a habitat helper.

Summary

Drawing a map is a good first step in planning changes or additions that will create or restore habitat for wildlife. To be a habitat helper, it is necessary to learn the specific needs for each species of animal to be able to offer the right combinations that will attract the most critters.

Following through

Contact the National Wildlife Federation, 1400 Sixteenth St., N.W., Washington, DC 20036-2266 to register your yard in their Official Backyard Habitat program. Suggest to your school's principal that a schoolyard conservation site be developed to restore an area of habitat for wildlife and create an outdoor learning center.

Imagine you are a real-estate agent and wild animals are your clients. Create a home video highlighting the "best of your backyard" as a selling tool to prospective "buyers."

HABITAT HELPERS CHECKLIST

Urban explorer's name _____   Date _____

What animals do you want to attract to your backyard?
Check off what you want to add to create or restore habitat for those animals.

	songbirds	butterflies	other insects	hummingbirds	bats	others
PLANTS						
Trees						
Shrubs						
Less lawn area						
Vegetable or herb garden areas						
Flower beds						
Trellis or arbor of vines						
Wildflower plantings						
Hummingbird nectar plants						
Butterfly larvae host plants						
Plants with berries, nuts, or fruits						
WILDLIFE PLACES						
Tree cavities						
Dead trees						
Burrows in the ground						
Hiding places (rock and brush piles/tall grass)						
Nesting areas						
Perching places						
Drinking places						
Bathing places						
Pond						
Bird feeders						
Bird houses						
Bat houses						
CONDITIONS						
Pesticide-free environment						
Quiet areas						
Protection from predators (pets)						

Critter castles

Subject
Science.

Science skills
Observing, recording, comparing, and contrasting.

Focus
Animals must find shelter within their habitat. What can people provide that offers shelter to critters?

Did you know?
The U.S. Forest Service says that over 400 wildlife species depend on dead, hollow, or fallen trees for food and family homes. Bluebirds make their nests in hollows of decaying trees, abandoned woodpecker holes, or rotten wooden fence posts. But bluebirds have declined in numbers because of a "housing shortage" as open fields with woodland edges have been developed by humans. Bluebirds have to compete with aggressive nonnative species such as sparrows and starlings for fewer natural cavity nest sites. In the 1970s, people concerned about the bluebird's plight began putting up bluebird houses to provide nesting sites to make up for those lost to human housing sites. Now bluebirds are making a comeback because of continued efforts made by people to provide them with shelter.

Bluebird in tree cavity

What you need
❑ Critter Castles Activity Sheet
❑ Pencil
❑ Natural materials (see the following)

Before you start
❑ Research animals in your area to discover their shelter needs.

What you do
1. Make a brush pile of fallen branches and woody plant trimmings. The pile will provide cover for birds, rabbits, and other small critters. Bugs, slugs, and snails that hide there might be food for birds and toads.

2. Construct a rock pile in a sunny corner. It might attract butterflies for sunning and give lizards a hunting and hiding place. Toads will burrow into the ground beneath a rock where it's cool and damp.

3. Build a bird house with a specific bird in mind. Birds are most picky about the diameter and placement of the entrance hole, and the depth, width, and height of the interior. For instance, a bluebird house should have a hole about the size of a quarter (1½"). This lets the bluebird in but discourages starlings. A depth of 6 inches from the hole to the floor of the house makes it harder for predators such as cats, starlings, and raccoons to reach the eggs or baby birds inside.

4. Contact your local wildlife agency to see about making a "bluebird trail." Many bluebird houses can be set up in a big circle or a long line. As a group project, people can watch over the houses weekly in spring and summer to assure bluebird nesting success.

5. Offer an assortment of bird nesting materials placed in wire baskets and hung in trees in the spring. "One-stop shopping" for items such as stuffing from old furniture, twigs, short pieces of yarn, or dog hair will save birds time and energy in collecting materials needed to make their nests.

6. Hang a basket of ferns or flowers on a deck or from a tree branch and watch to see if doves or house wrens make their nest in it.

7. Install a bat house. Plant nurseries, hardware stores, and nature centers sell them. It might take a while for bats to "rent" the new apartment, but once they do, they will provide payment by eating pesky mosquitoes.

8. "Plant" a 6- to 8-foot dead tree in your yard. Watch for woodpeckers, raccoons, owls, or opossums to take advantage of this disappearing habitat feature. Loose bark on dead trees also offers roosting sites for bats.

9. Attach a simple platform shelf to the side of your house under the eaves of the roof. This gives a weatherproof site for nesting robins, sparrows, eastern phoebes, and barn swallows.

10. Plant bushy shrubs, and mockingbirds, cardinals, and thrashers might build their nests there.

Summary

Natural areas with diverse plant life are the most attractive to wildlife, but in cities where those are lacking, families can create places where animals can seek shelter. Each wildlife species requires a unique blend of the four basic habitat needs. Learning just what they need and watching the behaviors of the critters that you want to seek shelter in your community will add up to success with critter castles. Inviting wildlife to live in your neighborhood provides enjoyment and environmental benefits such as insect pest control.

Following through

Make a "seeking-shelter" concentration game by photographing the following places in your neighborhood: potted plant saucer, eaves of a house, landscape timber, hole in a building, attic, bird house, hanging-plant basket, chimney, gravel rooftop, TV antennae, crack in cement wall, under a sidewalk, under a porch. Write the following wild places on 3.5"-×-5" index cards: pond, cliff overhang, under a log, tree holes, hollow trees, dense shrubbery, gravel riverbed, tree branches, crack in tree bark, under a rock, hollow log. Match the urban space cards to the wild place cards where animals seek shelter.

CRITTER CASTLES ACTIVITY SHEET

_____   _____
Urban explorer's name   Habitat

What shelters do you provide for wildlife?
As you create new critter castles, watch to see who moves in.
Record the number of critters observed using these shelters.

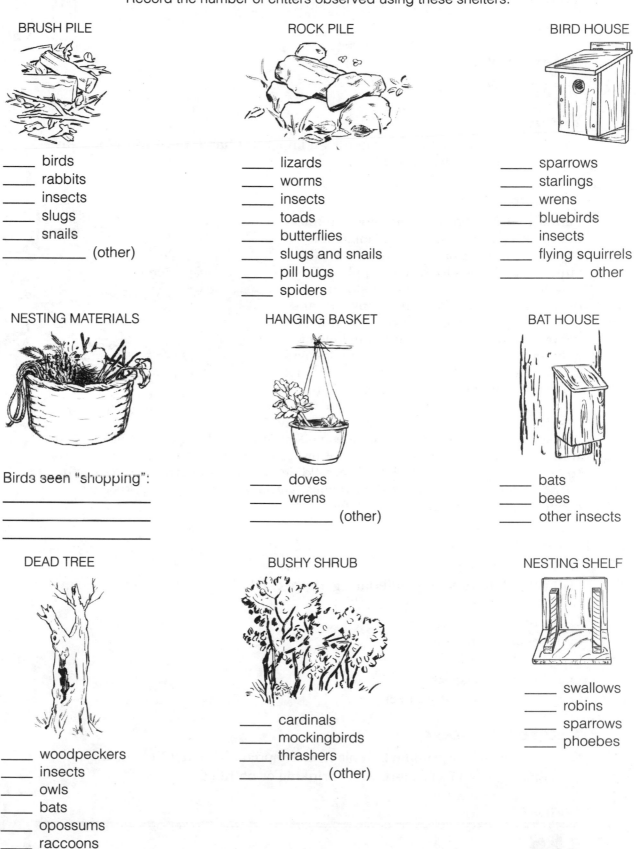

BRUSH PILE

____ birds
____ rabbits
____ insects
____ slugs
____ snails
_____ (other)

ROCK PILE

____ lizards
____ worms
____ insects
____ toads
____ butterflies
____ slugs and snails
____ pill bugs
____ spiders

BIRD HOUSE

____ sparrows
____ starlings
____ wrens
____ bluebirds
____ insects
____ flying squirrels
_____ other

NESTING MATERIALS

Birds seen "shopping":
_____
_____
_____

HANGING BASKET

____ doves
____ wrens
_____ (other)

BAT HOUSE

____ bats
____ bees
____ other insects

DEAD TREE

____ woodpeckers
____ insects
____ owls
____ bats
____ opossums
____ raccoons

BUSHY SHRUB

____ cardinals
____ mockingbirds
____ thrashers
_____ (other)

NESTING SHELF

____ swallows
____ robins
____ sparrows
____ phoebes

Water ways

Subject
Science.

Science skills
Observing, recording.

Focus
A consistent source of clean water is an important habitat feature. What ways can you provide water for wildlife?

Did you know?
Families make choices every day that affect the quality of water habitats. Household cleansers and old paint washed down the sink contaminate city water supplies. If used motor oil is poured down storm drains, it washes away with rainwater and pollutes aquatic habitats downstream. One gallon of motor oil can pollute millions of gallons of water. Grass clippings and leaves swept into storm drains get washed into local waterways. When the plant materials rot, they rob the water of oxygen. Lawn chemicals seep into ground water or run off into ponds, bayous,

Polluted water habitat

marshes, and lakes where pesticides poison animals. Fertilizers that reach the waterways cause too much algae to grow, and this imbalance in nature leads to a lack of oxygen in the water that wildlife needs. People can choose earth-friendly methods to care for their homes, yards, and cars to help keep water clean in natural settings for wildlife.

What you need
- ❏ Empty milk jug
- ❏ Bird bath or building materials (garbage can lid, tile drainage pipe, rock, string)
- ❏ Garden hose and water
- ❏ 1" rectangular cake pan
- ❏ Gravel
- ❏ String and scissors
- ❏ Water Ways Activity Sheet

Before you start
- ❏ Provide water for wildlife in a place where predators can't hide nearby. Animals like to feel secure while drinking or bathing.

WATER WAYS ACTIVITY SHEET

_____
Urban explorer's name

_____
Habitat

Add a variety of water sources to your other habitat ingredients.
What critters come to visit?

BIRD BATH
(home-made)

A garbage can lid placed upside down on a tile drainage
pipe is held in place by the weight of a rock tied to the
handle.

Animals observed: _____
_____
_____
_____
_____
_____

DRIPPING WATER

The container can drip into a shallow saucer or a bird bath.

Animals observed: _____
_____
_____
_____
_____
_____

TRICKLING WATER

Gravel on the bottom gives a more natural foothold for
birds.

Animals observed: _____
_____
_____
_____
_____

POND

Make it a minimum of 2 feet with gently sloping sides and
submerged rocks.

Animals observed: _____
_____
_____
_____
_____

What you do

1. Create an "artificial rain puddle." Buy a bird bath from the store or make one yourself using a stainless steel or plastic garbage can lid and a 3-foot ceramic drainage pipe (see activity sheet). The ideal size for a bird bath is 24–36" in diameter with gently sloping sides and a depth of no more than 3 inches. Roughly textured sides help birds get a grip. By raising the bird bath 3 feet off the ground, birds are safer from predators. Place the bird bath in the open. Birds might fly to a nearby bush if they feel threatened. Where do they preen and dry their feathers?

2. Dripping water attracts certain species, especially migratory birds such as warblers. Poke a tiny hole in the bottom corner of a clean, empty milk jug. Hang the jug by its handle with string from a branch. Fill it with water daily and let it drip into a shallow ceramic plant saucer on the ground.

3. For a trickling water source, hook up a hose and let it run slowly into a shallow cake pan. Put a layer of gravel on the bottom of the pan. Grow water-loving plants such as Louisiana iris, maidenhair fern, and cardinal flower nearby, since the area will probably stay moist.

4. Dig a pond. Any size will do, but a minimum depth of 2 feet allows for seasonal temperature variations and allows a variety of aquatic plants to grow there. Gently sloping sides offer a place for birds to wade in. A big rock submerged a few inches below the surface gives birds a spot to land on and bathe. Watch for toads, frogs, turtles, aquatic insects, and raccoons to join the pond community.

5. To keep the water clean, hose off and refill the water containers often. Even the pond might need to be cleaned sometimes. Never add chemicals to control algae.

6. Watch to see which animals are attracted to the different types of water sources. By just adding water to your list of habitat ingredients, what new critters came to visit?

Summary

Providing water in different ways is a valuable service to wildlife in the city. Puddles and ditches might dry up, especially in the heat of summer, so animals are attracted to a water source they can count on, and many of them become repeat customers.

Following through

Find out where your water supply comes from and take a tour of a water treatment facility in your town.

Critter cafeteria

Subject

Science.

Science skills

Comparing, contrasting, and predicting.

Focus

Open a restaurant for wildlife in your yard by growing native plants. How would you rate the menu in your backyard habitat if you were a city critter?

Did you know?

Native plants are ones that have evolved and occur naturally in your area. They are more closely matched to local soils, climate, and wildlife than exotic, imported plants. By using native plants and reducing lawn areas, people use less water, less pesticide, and less fertilizer, and people don't have to work as hard to maintain their yards.

What you need

❑ Critter Cafeteria Activity Sheet

❑ Seeds or cuttings from neighbors

❑ Native plants from a local nursery

What you do

1. Using the Critter Cafeteria Activity Sheet, rate the menu that is currently offered in your yard. What do you need to add to make it a "four-star" restaurant where "everyone who's anyone" will want to dine? Remember, the great thing about a cafeteria is the consistent variety of foods offered.

2. Contact a local nursery for suggestions of plants to add to the selections on your menu. Native plant societies often have seed swaps and meetings that will offer advice for plantings. Local nature centers are another source of plant lists that will have value for local wildlife throughout the seasons. Grow plants that produce fruits and flowers at different times of the year so that your restaurant does not run out of food.

3. Look to nature for examples of plant layering. Does your restaurant offer a canopy of trees, an understory, a shrub layer, and ground-level dining? Just as decor and appearances are important to people when they pick a restaurant, the arrangement of plants is important to wildlife. The more layers of landscaping, the more types of customers will come to your critter cafeteria.

4. Plant more than you think you will need because snails, slugs, and insects might come to dine, and they have big appetites. For pest control, rely on nature's predators or organic methods rather than using chemicals. Most birds, even seed-eaters, feed insects to their young, so birds are more likely to stay and nest in your yard when your menu is chemical-free and includes insects.

5. Offer "extra" menu items for special customers. Sugar-water feeders will satisfy hummingbirds, and feeders for seed-eaters will draw crowds.

6. Daily "specials" might include mushrooms on the lawn. Squirrels make a gourmet meal of them. Another treat for squirrels is an ear of corn.

Summary

Vegetation is the key to attracting most species of wildlife. Plants that are native to the area offer the most value to your local critter customers. Biodiversity is higher in habitats that include "four-star" critter cafeterias.

Following through

Make a bean-pole teepee in a sunny garden. Tie several long poles together at one end. Stand them up straight, and spread them out in a circle at the base. Push the poles into the ground. Plant scarlet runner beans at the base of each pole. When the plants cover the poles, it makes a shady place to play in. Bees get nectar and pollen from the flowers that later turn into beans, which provide food for birds and other animals, including people. Grow a sunflower playhouse by planting sunflower seeds in a big rectangle. Birds will eat the seeds on the "roof!"

CRITTER CAFETERIA ACTIVITY SHEET

_____
Urban explorer's name

_____
Date

How would critters rate the menu in your backyard habitat?

_____ 1 ★ = feeder only

_____ 2 ★ = feeder and water

_____ 3 ★ = feeder, water, and native plant foods

_____ 4 ★ = feeder, water, native plant foods, and insects in a chemical-free atmosphere

What do you need to do to your backyard to get a 4 ★ rating?

Good restaurants have a comfortable atmosphere as well as excellent food and beverage choices.

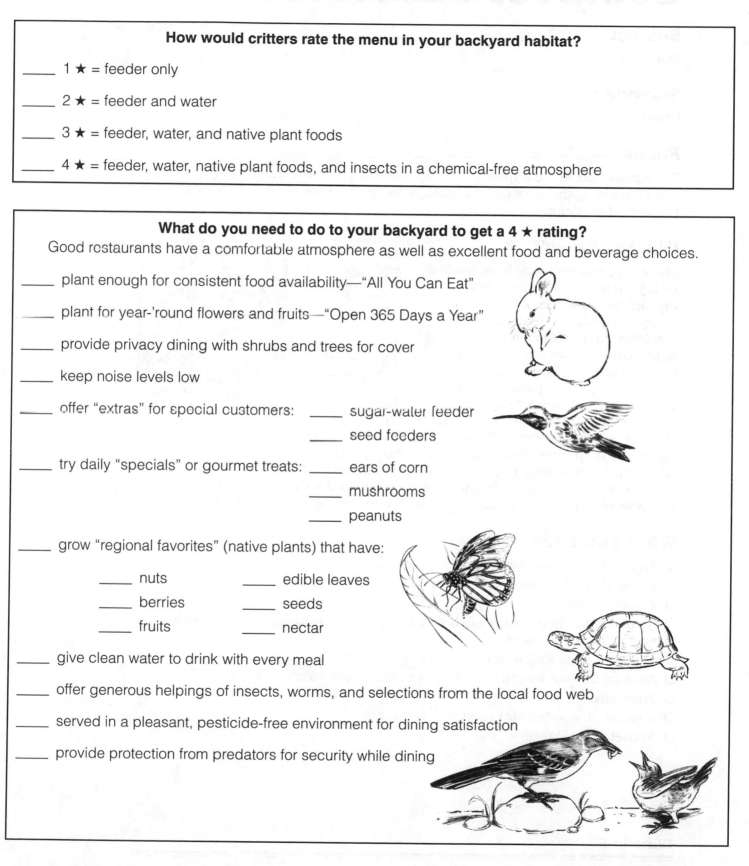

_____ plant enough for consistent food availability—"All You Can Eat"

_____ plant for year-'round flowers and fruits—"Open 365 Days a Year"

_____ provide privacy dining with shrubs and trees for cover

_____ keep noise levels low

_____ offer "extras" for special customers:
     _____ sugar-water feeder
     _____ seed feeders

_____ try daily "specials" or gourmet treats:
     _____ ears of corn
     _____ mushrooms
     _____ peanuts

_____ grow "regional favorites" (native plants) that have:

     _____ nuts   _____ edible leaves

     _____ berries   _____ seeds

     _____ fruits   _____ nectar

_____ give clean water to drink with every meal

_____ offer generous helpings of insects, worms, and selections from the local food web

_____ served in a pleasant, pesticide-free environment for dining satisfaction

_____ provide protection from predators for security while dining

Compost casserole

Subject
Science.

Science skill
Observing.

Concepts

Focus
Decomposition in a compost pile is nature's way of recycling nutrients so they can be used again. How do you make a compost casserole to feed hungry lawns and gardens?

Did you know?
Those big, black plastic bags stuffed with yard wastes at curbsides throughout America end up clogging landfills. Almost 20% of the solid waste collected in cities in the United States is made up of yard wastes. Composting leaves and grass clippings conserves landfill space. Many kitchen wastes can be added to compost to further reduce the strain on bulging landfills. Keeping these wastes out of landfills saves city taxpayers money in disposal costs. Some cities have community composting programs, but people with backyard compost piles have easy access to the dark, nutrient-rich, odorless soil conditioner that they can use in their gardens for free!

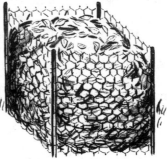

Composting yard wastes

What you need
- ❑ An armful of twigs and branches
- ❑ 1 bag of grass clippings
- ❑ 2 bags of leaves
- ❑ A bowl of kitchen scraps such as lettuce, coffee grounds, banana peels, eggshells, apple cores
- ❑ A garden hose and water
- ❑ About a 20-foot length of wire mesh (3 to 4 feet wide)
- ❑ Thin wire
- ❑ 4 metal or wooden stakes (3 to 4 feet long)
- ❑ Shovel or pitchfork

Before you start

❑ Pick a level area near a water source that gets about equal sun and shade.
❑ Dig up the grass in a 5-x-5 area so compost material will lay on top of soil. Save the grass patches.

What you do

1. To make your compost casserole "dish," drive stakes into the ground as supports for the wire sides of the compost pile. Stretch the wire mesh around the supports and wire it in place to the stakes. The size of your pile might depend on the size of your yard and the amount of yard wastes you have weekly. A pile that is 4 to 5 feet wide and high "cooks" well.

2. Add the first ingredient—twigs and small branches. Now dump in two bags of leaves.

3. Pile on a bag of grass clippings and throw in the kitchen scraps.

4. Inspect the saved grass patches. Are there soil and soil critters clinging to the roots? The soil microorganisms are important decomposer ingredients in the compost casserole. Add the grass patches next. Add a layer of soil.

5. Spray enough water on the compost layers to dampen.

6. If you have more of these ingredients, repeat the casserole layers by alternating the "brown" (leaves and woody materials) and "green" (kitchen scraps, grass clippings, plant trimmings).

   Baking tips:
   Water the pile every time it is turned or new ingredients are added.
   Do not add weeds, meats, dairy products, fatty scraps, grease, or bones.

7. After a few days, put a shovel into the middle and lift out some of the "baked goods." Are they hot? Some compost piles can reach temperatures of 160°F after only a few days!

8. Mix the compost casserole about every two weeks using the pitchfork. What critters can you observe living there? Did you see worms, pill bugs, slugs, and other decomposers at work?

9. The compost casserole is ready to feed to hungry lawns and gardens when it is dark, crumbly, and earthy-smelling. How long did it take to finish "baking?"

Summary

Using compost returns organic matter to the earth. As the plant materials break down, the pile gets smaller. The length of baking time for compost casseroles varies depending on the ingredients used and the outdoor temperatures. Contrary to popular belief, compost piles do not smell bad.

Compost casserole

Following through

Test the nutrient power of the composted material as a soil conditioner for gardening. Fill one pot with soil from your yard. Fill another pot with yard soil mixed half and half with compost material. Label each pot. Plant a seed ½" under the surface and water it. Place the pots in a sunny spot and see which one grows best. Add compost to a garden and transplant the growing plants outside.

Critter control

Subject
Science.

Science skill
Discovering cause and effect.

Focus
Gardening with too many chemicals can kill beneficial organisms living in the backyard community and be unhealthy for humans. What can you do to safely control pesky critters in your yard?

Did you know?
Rainwater washes pesticides from lawns and gardens into our water supplies. The combined effect of toxic chemicals used by many families on their yards can kill wildlife far from your hometown. Marshes and bays are nurseries for many aquatic creatures, so the balance of nature is very sensitive to the poisonous pollutants that run off from cities and towns upstream. Millions of pesticide containers end up in landfills and become a long-term environmental hazard.

Before you start
- ❏ Be aware that natural organic remedies might need to be applied more often, but insects do not become immune to them as they do to chemical ones.
- ❏ Avoid breathing in diatomaceous earth because the tiny, rough particles can irritate lungs and throats.
- ❏ Pyrethrum, a natural insecticide made from dried chrysanthemum flowers, has very low toxicity to animals. Always read the labels on pest control products for safe handling methods.

What you need
- ❏ Empty plastic spray bottles
- ❏ 1-gallon watering can or plastic bottle
- ❏ Dishwashing soap (low phosphate)
- ❏ Pyrethrum powder
- ❏ Diatomaceous earth
- ❏ Onion
- ❏ Garlic

- ❏ Red pepper
- ❏ Water
- ❏ Vinegar
- ❏ Permanent marker
- ❏ Bandannas

What you do

1. Gather kids together to form a conservation crew. Choose someone's backyard as a "demonstration site" for safe critter control methods. A container vegetable garden at school is a good site.

2. Make a critter control kit containing ready-to-use natural critter control materials. Using empty plastic spray bottles salvaged from the recycling bin, make up these two recipes:

    Label: Soap-and-water spray (for aphid control)
    Mix 1 teaspoon of dishwashing liquid with 1 gallon of water and pour into spray bottles.

    Label: Herbal critter control spray (all-purpose). Blend or chop:
    1 cup of onion
    2 cloves of garlic
    2 cups of water
    3 Tbsp. of red pepper
    Strain and add 1 gallon of cold water. Let stand for 24 hours. Fill spray bottles. Insects have a good sense of smell. The herbal spray covers the naturally attractive odors of the plants you want to protect, and the insects will go elsewhere.

3. Ladybugs are the natural predators of aphids. Praying mantises are also beneficial insects because they eat garden pests. They can be purchased at nurseries and used seasonally in addition to the other materials in the critter control kit.

4. Purchase pyrethrum powder and diatomaceous earth from a gardening center and keep them in the critter control kit. Store several bandannas in the kit.

5. Now have the crew walk through the site with the conservation kit and practice the safe critter control methods. First, protect plants by applying the herbal spray.

6. Look for aphids sucking on plant stems. If found, use the soap-and-water spray directly on the insects to smother them.

7. If fire ants are in an area where children are likely to get stung, pour pyrethrum and a gallon of vinegar into the ant mound. Do this in early to midmorning when the ground is warm but not hot, and most of the colony will be just under the mound instead of deeper down.

8. If there are too many slugs and snails eating plants, use diatomaceous earth to control the population. Wearing a bandanna over your nose and

mouth, sprinkle diatomaceous earth in areas where slime trails have been seen.

9. To discourage roaches near the house, dust lightly with diatomaceous earth outdoors. Inside, dust lightly with boric acid or borax.

10. Store the critter control kit in a handy, dry place. Have kids teach others about the methods and environmental benefits they learned on the "demonstration site."

Summary

Long-term use of pesticides kills everything in the yard, even beneficial insects and microscopic organisms that work to keep the soil fertile. Without soil organisms such as earthworms, pill bugs, and tiny microbes, the soil needs more fertilizers and water to grow plants, which leads to the need for even more chemicals. By getting rid of insects, you are less likely to attract many other city critters such as nesting songbirds, lizards, and toads that depend on insects for a meal or to feed their young. The beauty of insects such as butterflies and moths will be missed in pesticide-treated areas. By growing native plants, there is less need for pest control because the plants are naturally more disease and pest resistant. People can help maintain the interdependent community of living things by using alternatives to toxic lawn and garden chemicals.

Following through

Experiment with the natural insect repellent qualities of some plants in your garden. Plant herbs as companions alongside vegetables and flowers. Garlic is a good general insect repellent, especially of stem-sucking aphids. To repel white flies and improve the taste of tomatoes, some gardeners plant basil nearby. Marigolds planted throughout a garden keep soil free of root-sucking nematode worms.

Critter care

Subject

Science, language arts.

Concepts

Science skills

Observing, discovering cause and effect.

Focus

While nature has ways of taking care of its own, sometimes people need to help. What should you do if you find an injured or orphaned wild animal?

Did you know?

There is a network of volunteers who are trained care givers for injured or orphaned critters. As rehabilitators, they work to release wild animals back to their natural habitats. By calling the International Wildlife Rehabilitation Coalition, you can find out who has a federal permit to help wildlife in your area. Your veterinarian might also know local "rehabbers" who can

Mockingbird feeding fledgling

help you decide if a critter needs care or not. While some young animals might appear to need help, they are really in "nature's training program." For instance, some baby birds, such as ducklings and killdeer, can take care of themselves as soon as they are hatched. Most others, including mockingbirds and blue jays, spend three days to a week on the ground being watched over and fed by their parents. This is a dangerous time because of predators, but the young are busy learning important survival skills from parents. Just keep your pets put up, and enjoy nature's show.

Before you start

❑ Any animal, especially if frightened or hurt, is capable of biting!

❑ Always have an adult handle a wild animal.

❑ Raccoons, skunks, and bats are considered high risk for rabies. Do not touch.

❑ Do not kidnap a healthy baby animal for a pet. Adult wild animals do not make good pets.

What you need

❑ A box with a lid

❑ A stick, broom, or shovel

❑ Paper bag

❑ Gloves

❑ Heating pad

CRITTER CARE GUIDE SHEET

_____   _____
Urban explorer's name   Date

Follow these guidelines if you find injured or orphaned wildlife.
It is illegal to possess wild animals without state and federal permits.

BIRDS

Tiny Baby Bird: If you can find the nest, put the baby back in. Since birds have a poor sense of smell, they will not know you've handled it. If there is no nest, keep the baby warm and contained and get help.

Small Fledgling Bird: If the parent is around, leave the bird alone. Put pets up. Put it in a hanging basket in a tree if a neighbor's cat is stalking. If it is hurt or the mother doesn't come all day, keep it warm and contained and get help.

Injured Adult Bird with a Large Beak: Wear sunglasses to protect your eyes when handling herons, owls, hawks, and woodpeckers. Use caution when putting in a box. Call for help.

Injured Adult Songbird: Pick up carefully, keep warm and contained and call for help.

MAMMALS
Adult squirrels, rabbits, and opossums can bite, even through heavy gloves.

Baby Squirrel: They are born blind and without fur. Put the baby in a shoe box off the ground away from ants. If the mother does not come or it is injured, keep it warm and contained and call for help.

Rabbit: If it is 4–5 inches long, it is old enough to be on its own. If it is in danger from your pet, take it to a safer, suitable habitat. If it is tiny or injured, keep it warm and contained and get help.

Bat: If a bat flies in your house, leave a window open but close the door of that room. At dusk, it will fly out. An injured or sick bat found outside should not be touched.

Opossum: If it is 7–8 inches long (not counting the tail), it is old enough to be on its own. If it is tiny or injured, keep it warm and contained and get help.

REPTILES
Do not touch any snake that you are not absolutely sure is nonvenomous. All snakes can bite.

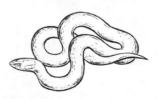

Lizards, Turtles, and Snakes: These animals are on their own as soon as they hatch from eggs. Leave them alone. If injured, keep warm in a box and get help.

Adult Turtles: They can bite! Wear gloves or use a shovel to pick up. Put in a container, keep warm, and get help.

- ❑ Towel
- ❑ Sunglasses
- ❑ International Wildlife Rehabilitation Coalition phone, (707) 864-1761
- ❑ Critter Care Guide Sheet

What you do

1. Prepare a critter care kit by gathering the supplies on the "what you need" list and putting them in the cardboard box.

2. On the inside of the box lid, make a checklist by writing the following steps:
   - Have an adult pick up the wild animal safely, if it needs help. A towel might need to be thrown over the animal to catch it. Wearing gloves, push the animal into a box or paper bag with a stick or broom. Put in some tissue or cotton and tape the top closed.
   - Keep the animal warm. The container might be placed half on and half off a heating pad that is turned on a "low" setting.
   - To keep the animal calm, avoid loud noises from radio and television. The darkness in the container will also make the critter feel more secure.
   - Do not feed the animal food or water. The wrong foods can do more harm than good. Water that goes down the wrong way in a bird's throat can drown it.

3. Look up the phone number of a veterinarian. Call the International Wildlife Rehabilitation Coalition for the number of a local rehabilitation group. Write the phone numbers on the box.

4. Copy the Critter Care Guide Sheet and keep it in the box so the critter care kit is ready to be used the next time a wild animal needs help in your neighborhood.

Summary

As cities and towns grow, wild animals are forced to live nearer to people. Sometimes these close encounters cause problems for critters and the people. A dove, seeing only blue sky reflected, might fly into a shiny window on your house. A turtle might be hit by a car as it travels to the next pond. A family pet might get in a fight and injure a raccoon. A well-meaning family that tries to care for an orphaned baby bird will soon find that the newborn bird might need to eat every 15 minutes! Trained volunteers know how, what, and when to feed injured or orphaned animals, which increases the chances for successful release of the animal. Caring for critters helps nurture nature close to home.

Following through

Volunteer for organizations that care for critters.

Suggested books

Ajilvsgi, Geyata. 1990. *Butterfly Gardening for the South*. Dallas: Taylor Publishing Company.

> This book tells you all about the fascinating world of butterflies—their lifestyles, feeding habits, and how to plan your backyard to attract butterflies.

Beatley, Timothy. 1994. *Habitat Conservation Planning*. Austin, Tex.: University of Texas Press.

> This is a good book to read if you want to learn more in-depth facts about the possibility of urban development being done appropriately for wildlife.

Dew, Tina, and Curtis and Reber Layton. 1986. *Bluebirds*. Jackson, Miss.: Nature Books Publishers.

> A book about the daily lives of bluebirds and how to attract and raise them.

Hodge, Guy R. 1991. *Pocket Guide to the Humane Control of Wildlife in Cities and Towns*. Mont.: Falcon Press.

> This small guide put out by The Humane Society of the United States has many good ideas on how to share your habitat with wildlife safely and humanely.

Martin, Deborah L. and Grace Gershuny. 1992. *The Rodale Book of Composting*. Emmaus, Pa.: Rodale Press.

> Never composted before? This book will tell you how.

Sheehan, K. and M. Waldner. 1991. *Earthchild*. Tulsa, Okla.: Council Oaks Books.

> The activities in this book teach an earth-nurturing attitude.

Tuttle, Merlin D. 1988. *America's Neighborhood Bats*. Austin, Tex.: University of Texas Press.

> A book designed to teach you how to understand and learn to live in harmony with bats; it includes a design for a bat house.

Resource list

The following is a list of conservation organizations and materials:

Bat Conservation International
P.O. Box 162603
Austin, TX 78716
512-327-9721

Nonprofit organization that promotes bat conservation projects worldwide; offers a catalog of educational materials and gift items ranging from jewelry to bat houses.

Carolina Biological Supply Company
2700 York Rd.
Burlington, NC 27215
800-334-5551

Mail-order supplier of science education materials.

Center for Environmental Education
881 Alma Real Dr.
Suite 300
Pacific Palisades, CA 90272
310-454-4585

A nonprofit organization with a comprehensive K–12 environmental resource and curricula library, including the publication *Blueprint for a Green School*.

Connecticut Valley Biological Supply Company
P.O. Box 326
Southampton, MA 01073
800-355-6813

Mail-order supplier of science education materials.

Cornell Lab of Ornithology
159 Sapsucker Woods Rd.
Ithaca, NY 14850
607-254-2473

An international center that enlists volunteers to collect information for the study and conservation of birds; offers a catalog of educational materials, birder gift items, binoculars, and bird feeders.

International Wildlife Rehabilitation Coalition

4437 Central Place Suite B-4
Suisun, CA 94585
707-864-1761 (in Texas, call 713-468-8972)

A nonprofit organization that offers training to a network of volunteers who care for and release orphaned and injured wildlife.

National Audubon Society

700 Broadway
New York, NY 10003-9501
212-979-3000

Conservation, education, political, and citizen action nonprofit group that is dedicated to protecting habitats with an emphasis on birds and threatened ecosystems.

National Institute for Urban Wildlife

P.O. Box 3015
Sheperdstown, WV 25443
304-876-6146

A nonprofit organization that provides practical educational information for control, maintenance, or enhancement of wildlife populations in urban and developing areas.

National Wildflower Research Center

2600 FM 973 N.
Austin, TX 78725
512-929-3600

A nonprofit organization that serves as a national clearinghouse of information about native plants, their sources, and uses in public and private landscaping.

National Wildlife Federation

1400 16th St. N.W.
Washington, DC 20036-2266
202-797-6800

A nonprofit organization that educates and assists people in conservation efforts for wildlife and other natural resources throughout the world. Outstanding publications include: *Annual Conservation Directory* (item #79562). Call 1-800-432-6564 to order this comprehensive list of organizations, agencies, and officials concerned with natural resource use and management; *NatureScope*, a magazine full of educational activities for kids; *Backyard Habitat Program,* an official certification and helpful guide to creating habitats for wildlife.

Partners in Flight

National Fish and Wildlife Foundation
1120 Connecticut Ave. N.W.
Suite 900
Washington, DC 20036

An international nonprofit organization that combines resources and educational materials from many cooperating conservation groups and governmental agencies to preserve habitat for migratory birds.

Project WILD

P.O. Box 18060
Boulder, CO 80308-8060
303-444-2390

An interdisciplinary environment and conservation education program for educators of K–12th grade.

Project Learning Tree

American Forest Foundation
1111 19th Street, N.W.
Washington, DC 20036

A comprehensive environmental education activity guide for grades K–8 is offered by this organization.

Purple Martin Conservation Association

Edinboro University of Pennsylvania
Edinboro, PA 16444
814-734-4420

An international nonprofit organization that does research and education to conserve purple martins throughout their range; offers a colony registry program and a catalog of purple martin products.

Real Goods

966 Mazzoni St.
Ukiah, CA 95482-3471
800-762-7325

A mail-order source for worms and worm bins.

The Peregrine Fund

5666 W. Flying Hawk Ln.
Boise, ID 83709
208-362-8687

A nonprofit group that assists in conservation projects worldwide as well as being involved in peregrine falcon and other bird species restoration to habitats in North America.

Young Entomologist Society
1915 Peggy Place
Lansing, MI 48910-2553
517-887-0499

A nonprofit organization that offers educational publications, programs, and insect specimen exchange among members.

Wildseed Farms, Inc.
P.O. Box 308
Eagle Lake, TX 77434
800-848-0078

Catalog source for seeds of wildflowers and herbs.

Wildscapes: Nongame and Urban Program
Texas Parks and Wildlife Department
4200 Smith School Road
Austin, TX 78744

Backyard and schoolyard habitat program that offers educational materials and start-up advice.

Glossary

adaptation A special feature or behavior of an organism that improves its chances of survival and reproduction.

community A group of interdependent living things in a habitat.

conservation The wise use of natural resources in a way that assures they will continue to be available to future generations.

ecology The scientific study of the relationships of living things to one another and to their environment.

ecosystem The system in which living and nonliving things on earth interact.

endangered animal or plant A species whose numbers are declining and that is in danger of becoming extinct throughout all or much of its range.

environment The living and nonliving surroundings in which a plant or animal lives.

extinct A species of plant or animal that has no individuals left alive on earth.

fledgling A young bird between the time of hatching and first flight.

food chain The transfer of food energy from one living thing to another in a sequence in which each member of the chain feeds on the one below it.

habitat The place that provides food, shelter, water, and space for an animal or plant to live.

instinct A response by an organism to its environment that does not involve reasoning and is passed from generation to generation.

micro-habitat A small habitat within a larger one in which moisture, light, and other conditions differ from those in the surrounding area.

natural resources Raw materials and energy available from the earth, such as nutrients, water, minerals, plants, and animals.

niche The role that a species has in nature; its job within its habitat.

organic matter Made of living and dead organisms.

organism Any living thing.

pollination The transfer of pollen from the male part of the plant (anther) to the female part (stigma) of the same plant or to another plant of the same species.

seed The part of a plant that contains the embryo and will develop into a new plant.

shelter Something that provides protection from weather or danger.

species A group of living things made up of related individuals that resemble one another and are able to breed among themselves, but are not able to breed with members of another species.

threatened animal or plant A species that is likely to become endangered because of a decline in numbers.

Bibliography

Arnosky, Jim. 1983. *Secrets of a Wildlife Watcher.* New York: Lothrop, Lee and Shepard.

Farrand, John. 1985. *The Audubon Society's Master Guide to Birding.* New York: Alfred A. Knopf.

Garber, Steven D. 1987. *The Urban Naturalist.* New York: John Wiley and Sons, Inc.

Heilman, Joan R. 1983. *Bluebird Rescue.* New York: Lothrop, Lee and Shepard.

Hutchins, Ross E. 1967. *The Ant Realm.* New York: Dodd, Mead and Co.

Imes, Rick. 1992. *The Practical Entomologist.* New York: Simon and Schuster.

Kress, Stephen W. 1981. *The Audubon Society's Handbook for Birders.* New York: Charles Scribner and Sons.

Kress, Stephen W. 1991. *Bird Life.* New York: Golden Press.

Landry, Sarah. 1994. *Peterson First Guide to Urban Wildlife.* Boston: Houghton Mifflin Co.

Mac Clintock, Dorcas. 1981. *A Natural History of Raccoons.* New York: Charles Scribner and Sons.

Martin, Alexander C., Herbert S. Zim and Arnold L. Nelson. 1951. *American Wildlife and Plants.* New York: Dover Publications.

Nabham, Gary P. and Stephen Trimble. 1994. *The Geography of Childhood: Why Children Need Wild Places.* Boston: Beacon Press.

Overbeck, Cynthia. 1982. *Ants.* Minneapolis: Lerner Publications.

Quinn, John R. 1994. *Wildlife Survivors: The Flora and Fauna of Tomorrow.* Blue Ridge Summit, Pa.: TAB/McGraw-Hill.

Stokes, Donald W. 1983. *A Guide to Observing Insect Lives.* Boston: Little, Brown and Co.

Stokes, Donald W., Lillian Q. Stokes and Ernest Williams. 1991. *The Butterfly Book.* Boston: Little, Brown and Co.

Thompson, Gerald and Jennifer Coldrey, 1984. *The Pond.* Cambridge, Mass.: MIT Press.

Tufts, Craig. 1993. *The Backyard Naturalist.* Washington, D.C.: National Wildlife Federation.

Wright, Rachel. 1989. *Look at Eyes, Ears, and Noses.* New York: Franklin Watts.

Wright, Robert H. 1971. *Curious Ways of Common Birds.* New York: Lothrop, Lee and Shepard.

Zim, Herbert S. and Clarence Cottam. 1991. *Insects: A Guide to Familiar American Insects.* New York: Golden Press.

Index

A

activities
  amphibian observation, 80-83
  Backyard Habitat Program, 121
  backyard observations, 94-96
  bee observation, 111-113
  bird feeding and observing, 114-116
  bird watching, 41-43
  care kit, critter, 138-140
  comparison of diverse areas, 53-55
  compost casserole, 132-134
  crayfish hunt, 84-86
  crustacean habitat, 103
  describing nature, 12-14
  food finding, 38-40
  habitat helper, 120-122
  habitat hunt, 26-28
  insect habitats, 100-103
  insect investigations, 60-62
  journal, listening, 4
  leaf identification, 97-99
  leaf-rubbing, 99
  listening to nature, 3-6
  map drawing, 121
  messy day, 16
  metamorphosis, 107-110
  micro-hiking, 56-60
  migrating bird, 29-31
  navigating by touch, 15-16
  ornithology, 41-43
  pest control, 135-137
  pH of water, 73
  plant pursuit game, 35-37
  pond
    exploration, 70-72
    life observation, 76-79
  purposes of creatures, 44-46
  reading about animals, 5
  restaurant for animals, 129-131
  seed observation, 32-34
  sensory experiences, 20-22
  shelters for animals, 123
  smelling for survival, 17-19
  soil sampler, 63-65
  stalking, 7-9
  teepee, bean-pole, 130
  touch and learn, 10-11
  tracks, locating and identifying, 87-90
  urban exploration, 50-52
  video, 121
  water
    sampler, 73-75
    providing, 126-128
  worm world, 104-106
amphibians, 80-83
animals
  amphibians, 80-83
  bats, 6, 20
  behavioral differences, 5, 87
  benefits of, 44
  birds (*see* birds)
  camouflage, 14
  cats, 13
  consumers, 56-60
  coyotes, 13
  crustaceans, 84-86, 100-103
  decomposers, 56-60
  eyes, 13-14
  foxes, 7
  frogs, 80-83
  insects (*see* insects)
  isopods, 100-103
  moles, 15, 63
  newborns, 138-140
  producers, 56-60
  rabbits, 3, 37
  raccoons, 10
  reading about, 5
  seasons, 5-6
  snakes, 14
  squirrels, 37
  toads, 80-83
  worms (*see* worms)
ants, 19
Audubon Society, 114

B

bacteria, 63
bats, 6, 20
bees, 111-113

behavioral differences in animals, 5, 87
biodiversity, 40, 49, 73-75, 78
birds, 6, 12, 20, 26, 28, 29, 37, 41-43, 114-116
  Audubon Society, 114
  bluebirds, 123
  bluejays, 114
  cardinals, 114
  falcons, 26, 28
  golden-cheeked warblers, 120
  goldfinches, 114
  hummingbirds, 29
  robins, 41
bluebirds, 123
bluejays, 114
botanists, 32
butterflies, 107-110

C
camouflage, 12, 14, 60
canopies, 55
cardinals, 114
caterpillars, 107-110
cats, 13
cities,
  food sources, 29
  history of, 25
  shelter, 28
compost, 132-134
consumers, 56-60
coyotes, 13
crustaceans, 84-86, 100-103

D
damselflies, 70
decomposers, 56-60
dragonflies, 70, 72

E
earthworms, 63, 104-106
echo-location, 20
ecotourism, 52
entomologist, 60
environment
  awareness of the, 52
  landfills, 132-134
  recycling trash, 132-134

F
falcons, peregrine, 26-28
fireflies, 50
flocking, 43
food chain, 40, 59
footprints, animal, 87-90
foresters, urban, 53
foxes, 7
frogs, 80-83
fungi, 63

G
gills, 100-103
golden-cheeked warblers, 120
goldfinches, 114
grasshoppers, 6

H
houseflies, 56
hummingbirds, 29

I
insects, 63-65
  ants, 19
  bees, 111-113
  benefits of, 44, 113
  butterflies, 107-110
  camouflage, 12, 14, 60
  caterpillars, 107-110
  damselflies, 70
  dragonflies, 70, 72
  entomologist, 60
  eyes, compound, 13-14
  fireflies, 50
  grasshoppers, 6
  habitats, 100-103
  houseflies, 56
  investigating, 60-62
  leaf hoppers, 14
  maggots, 56
  metamorphosis, 107-110
  monarch butterflies, 62
  moths, 17, 60
  oleander moth, 60
  pesticides, 137
  pollination, 111
  snails, 13-14
  spiders, 6
  syrphid flies, 12
  whirligig beetle, 76
International Wildlife Rehabilitation Coalition,
    138
isopods, 100-103

J
journal, listening, 4

L
leaf hoppers, 14

M
maggots, 56
metamorphosis, 107-110
migration, 28, 30
milkweed, 62
moles, 15, 63
monarch butterflies, 62
moths, 17, 60

N

National Wildlife Federation, 121
newborns, 138-140

O

oleander moth, 60
oronthology, 41-43
organizations, wildlife
  Audubon Society, 114
  International Wildlife Rehabilitation
    Coalition, 138
  National Wildlife Federation, 121
  U.S. Forest service, 123
overstory canopy, 55

P

peregrine falcons, 26, 28
pesticide, 26, 50, 135-137
pheromones, fake, 17
photosynthesis, 97
plants
  aquatic, 72
  insect habitats, 100-103
  leaf identification, 97-99
  milkweed, 62
  native, 129-130
  overstory canopy, 55
  photosynthesis, 97
  poisonous, 37, 97
  pollination, 111
  seed dispersal, 35-37
  shrub layer, 55
  soil producers, 32
  understory canopy, 55
  violets, 37
poisonous plants, 37, 97
pollination, 111

pond
  definition of, 76
  zones, 77
producers, 56-60

R

rabbits, 3, 37
raccoons, 10
robins, 41

S

seasons, 5-6
shrub layer, 55
snails, snakes 13-14
soil, 32, 63-65, 134
spiders, 6
squirrels, 37
syrphid flies, 12

T

toads, 80-83
tracks, animal, 87-90
trash, recycling, 132-134

U

understory canopy, 55
U.S. Forest Service, 123
urban foresters, 53

W

whirligig beetle, 76
worms
  earthworms, 63, 104-106
  habitat of, 104-106
  tubiflex, 73

V

violets, 37

About the authors

Janet Wier Roberts is a nature education consultant who has designed Discovery Boxes with hands-on activities for nature centers around the United States. As a volunteer trail guide for the Houston Arboretum & Nature Center, she has experience using their innovative programs and activities with school children. She also teaches conservation and ecology to middle schoolers at a private school in Houston, where students are involved in creating wildlife habitat on school grounds by growing native plants.

Carole Huelbig, a certified teacher with more than 20 years of experience, has worked as a naturalist at the Houston Arboretum & Nature Center for 15 years. She leads school and scout tours through the urban forest and plans and teaches programs for 5- to 12-year-olds. She is responsible for the development of hands-on, self-paced exhibits in the nature center's Discovery Room, which teach about habitats for wildlife.

Other Bestsellers
of Related Interest

Nature through Science and Art
—Susie Gwen Criswell
A how-to book for teachers, parents, and other educators who spend time exploring nature with children. Instills a deep awareness of the environment in children in grades 3-6 through hands-on science investigations and art activities.

0-07-013783-8   **$12.95 Paper**
0-07-013782-X   **$22.95 Hard**

Kids Can Make a Difference!: Environmental Science Activities
—H. Steven Dashefsky
Fun and challenging activities and projects in environmental science that allow students to explore real-world environmental problems and to investigate their possible solutions.

0-07-015747-2   **$12.95 Paper**
0-07-015746-4   **$19.95 Hard**

Make an Interactive Science Museum: Hands on Exhibits
—Robert Gardner
Robert Gardner's project guide to making your own science museum for kids.

0-07-022867-1   **$16.95 Paper**

Super Science Fair Sourcebook
—Maxine Haren Iritz
Dozens of projects, with prize-winning tips from concept to presentation, make this book the ideal resource for science fair entries in grades six through nine.

0-07-032849-8   **$21.95 Paper**

How to Order

Call 1-800-822-8158
24 hours a day,
7 days a week
in U.S. and Canada

Mail this coupon to:
McGraw-Hill, Inc.
P.O. Box 182067
Columbus, OH 43218-2607

Fax your order to:
614-759-3644

EMAIL
70007.1531@COMPUSERVE.COM
COMPUSERVE: GO MH

Shipping and Handling Charges

Order Amount	Within U.S.	Outside U.S.
Less than $15	$3.50	$5.50
$15.00 - $24.99	$4.00	$6.00
$25.00 - $49.99	$5.00	$7.00
$50.00 - $74.49	$6.00	$8.00
$75.00 - and up	$7.00	$9.00

EASY ORDER FORM—
SATISFACTION GUARANTEED

Ship to:

Name _____

Address _____

City/State/Zip _____

Daytime Telephone No. _____

Thank you for your order!

ITEM NO.	QUANTITY	AMT.

Method of Payment:

☐ Check or money order enclosed (payable to McGraw-Hill)

☐ DISCOVER   ☐ AMERICAN EXPRESS Cards

☐ VISA   ☐ MasterCard

Shipping & Handling charge from chart below	
Subtotal	
Please add applicable state & local sales tax	
TOTAL	

Account No. ☐☐☐☐☐☐☐☐☐☐☐☐☐☐☐☐

Signature _____ Exp. Date _____
Order invalid without signature

**In a hurry? Call 1-800-822-8158 anytime,
day or night, or visit your local bookstore.**

Key = BC95ZZA